The Critics Were
Wrong _____

The Critics Were
Wrong ‚Äî‚Äî‚Äî‚Äî

Misguided Movie Reviews and Film Criticism Gone Awry

ARDIS SILLICK AND MICHAEL MCCORMICK

With an Introduction by ED GORMAN

A CITADEL PRESS BOOK
Published by Carol Publishing Group

Frontispiece: Robert DeNiro as Jake LaMotta in *Raging Bull*

Copyright © 1996 by Ardis Sillick and Michael McCormick

A Citadel Press Book
Published by Carol Publishing Group
Citadel Press is a registered trademark of Carol Communications, Inc.
Editorial Offices: 600 Madison Avenue, New York, N.Y. 10022
Sales and Distribution Offices: 120 Enterprise Avenue, Secaucus, N.J. 07094
In Canada: Canadian Manda Group, One Atlantic Avenue, Suite 105, Tornoto, Ontario M6K 3E7
Queries regarding rights and permissions should be addressed to Carol Publishing Group, 600 Madison Avenue, New York, N.Y. 10022

Carol Publishing Group books are available at special discounts for bulk purchases, sales promotion, fund-raising, or educational purposes. Special editions can be created to specifications. For details contact: Special Sales Department, Carol Publishing Group, 120 Enterprise Avenue, Secaucus, N.J. 07094

Manufactured in the United States of America

10 9 8 7 6 5 4 3 2 1

Library of Congress Cataloging-in-Publication Data

Sillick, Ardis.
    The critics were wrong : misguided movie reviews and film criticism gone awry / Ardis Sillick, Michael McCormick.
        p.   cm.
    "A Citadel Press book."
    ISBN 0-8065-1722-0 (pbk.)
    1. Motion pictures—Reviews.   2. Motion pictures—Evaluation.
I. McCormick, Michael, 1947– . II. Title.
PN1995..S49375 1996
791.43'75—dc20   95-19782
                                                                  CIP

For Helen and Maxene

Acknowledgments ⸺⸺⸺⸺⸺

We would like to thank friends and family for their support, John McCarty for his advice and generosity, and Mark Cuthbertson for his time and patience. We would also like to acknowledge the library aides at the University of Iowa and the University of Northern Iowa, for whom we left those piles of bound periodicals and rolls of microfilm to reshelve.

And our thanks to the studios that produced the movies for permission to use the photos in this book.

Contents _____

Introduction ──────────────

He is invariably called a middlebrow by the sort of middlebrow whose idea of a highbrow is an academic.

—Fran Lebowitz in her introduction to the Modern Library edition of John O'Hara's *Appointment in Samara.*

I

This book is about some people who said some very foolish things and were nice enough to say them in print so we can savor them over and over again.

I'm talking about certain movie reviewers who spend far too much of their time slashing, bashing, and trashing too many of the films that come their way.

Now understand me: Some film reviewers and critics are very useful. Virtually every issue of *Film Comment*, for example, offers readers first-rate pieces on careers, vogues, and trends, on actors overlooked, pictures too long scorned, and screenwriters who weren't beboozed hacks after all.

But I don't read just learned journals. I find useful reviews in all kinds of magazines. Just this afternoon, for instance, I read a very stylish and cogent review of the new director's cut of *Sam Peckinpah's The Wild Bunch*. It was an appreciation written by Tom Gliatto and appeared in *People* magazine.

But you'll find nothing remotely resembling that kind of sagaciousness in the book at hand. No, what we have

before us are nothing but *negative* reviews. Some are so
seething with scorn it's a wonder they didn't lead to a few
suicides on the part of the poor actors and actresses
being trashed. What *The Critics Were Wrong* offers is the
remark most intemperate, the jibe most untutored, the
thrust most fey and inane, in other words, reviewers
trying to convince us that they really are wonderful and
dazzling creatures after all. The term we want here is
showing off—that's what these boys and girls do best. If
they're not hissing insults they're parading their would-
be erudition.

II

I sold my first novel in 1984, and when it appeared, in
the late summer of 1985, my editor sent me the first three
reviews. Two were quite good. One ended by saying that
my novel "was one of the most auspicious debuts of the
year." The third review was horrible, really vicious, and
said not a single complimentary thing about my book at
all. In fact, the last line was: "Definitely not
recommended."

Somehow the glow of those first two reviews faded,
and soon enough all I could remember—or think about
for some time—was that terrible review I'd received.
Despite a few dozen very positive reviews, I still remember my first book as critically tainted because of that
lone bad notice.

A few years later I saw a famous actor on a talk show.
The host brought up the subject of reviews and the actor
said, "You want to talk about reviews. Listen to this." And
he then proceeded to quote, from memory, a long and
savage review he'd recently received from a major news-
paper. He laughed about it, but I could see that it was

pained laughter. And then he said something that seems to be true for most of us who act or write or direct or dance or paint or sculpt or sing or play an instrument professionally: "I remember the bad reviews," the actor noted, "a lot longer than I remember the good ones." This isn't really a complaint. When you write books, or get up on stage and act, or conduct a symphony, you're going to be evaluated and inevitably be criticized. That's part of the process, part of the game. But one may wish for more civility on the part of certain reviewers, and for less showing off when they come to assess a given piece of work.

Some people seem able to laugh off bad reviews. Others are seriously damaged by them.

One novelist I know pretends to dismiss them entirely. It becomes a kind of machismo, the way he claims not to take them seriously. I know a psychotherapist who writes suspense novels who gives himself a formal three-day mourning period whenever he gets a notably terrible review. And I know a female mystery novelist who believes every negative word a given critic says about her. Her friends spend days reassuring her that she really *is* a fine, worthwhile, and popular writer. And you know the hell of it? She really is all these things, and a damned fine person to boot. I hate to see her so deeply affected by reviews—but to be honest, I don't handle the really bad ones all that well, either.

I was a reviewer myself for several years, and while I was never a hatchet man, I certainly wrote things I now wish had never been published. Foolish, foolish things.

Today when I buy reviews for *Mystery Scene*, a magazine I edit, I have one cardinal rule: It's fair to say that you didn't care for a particular piece of work, but it's not fair to use the review as a personal attack.

When a friend calls me depressed about a critical drubbing he or she has just received, I always say the same thing: "No matter how bad our books may be, they'll be around a lot longer than most of the reviews."

When Ardis and Mike were putting this book together, they had to spend years gathering the reviews because reviews can only be found on scratchy microfilm or dusty shelves.

Then consider most of the movies and actors trashed by the critics in this book. Many, if not most of them, can easily be found in video stores or through video mail-order houses. Unlike the reviews, the works themselves are readily available. These movies, despite the critical attacks they may have received, have endured for a simple reason—they deserved to endure. They have some quality, or qualities, that the reviewers failed to discern or appreciate.

Too many reviewers argue as if they've been commissioned by the Vatican to smite bad art wherever it appears. You find a lot of self-righteousness and pomposity in their remarks. It's this that looks especially silly down the years. Note some of the remarks made about the early Robert De Niro—the reviewers sound as if they're trying to work up a lynch mob.

Sartre argued that almost all important art comes from the highbrow or the lowbrow, and I certainly agree with that. Yet too many of our truly influential reviewers are, in every respect, middlebrow. If you doubt me, count the number of *mea culpas* being visited upon Sam Peckinpah these days. Twenty-five years later, because the highbrows vindicated him, the middlebrow reviewing establishment now says it's all right to like Peckinpah's movies. Smart people knew that 30 years ago, when they first saw one of the great American classics, Peckinpah's *Ride the High Country*.

III

There are certainly some wonderfully daft reviews to be found in this gloriously readable book. According to various critics, people such as Ingmar Bergman, Lauren Bacall, Robert De Niro, Nicholas Cage, and many others had no hope of movie careers at all. They can't even find kind words for *Annie Hall*, *Chinatown*, or *La Dolce Vita*.

To be sure, not all reviewers agreed with these dour judgments, but it is amazing to look through the reviews of masterpieces.

To repeat what I said earlier: I find many reviewers worth reading, and quite helpful. Roger Ebert, whom I knew slightly during our teen years, can be an incisive and valuable guide through the maze of "video product" that confronts us these days. I would say the same of Andrew Sarris and William K. Everson, Richard Schickel, Richard Corliss, and Jack Kroll, sometimes David Denby, and almost always Janet Maslin, even when I disagree with her. And the same with Molly Haskell. These folks seem to genuinely like movies. They're not grad school twits or fast-guns who make their reputations by trying to humiliate actors, directors, and writers.

But why anybody would pay attention to reviewers such as John Simon, (the Mr. Blackwell of movie critics)—you got me. The remarks he's made about the physical appearance of certain actresses are unforgivable. A real gentleman would punch him out for writing things so ungallant.

Suspense fiction, which is what I write, was once graced by a fine critic named Anthony Boucher who, for almost two decades, was the mystery critic for the *New York Times*. He was a superb critic, open to all the varieties of the crime novel. When Boucher died the *Times* appointed an erudite and generally even-handed reviewer named Alan J. Hubin to cover mysteries. (I say even-handed despite the fact that he once disemboweled a novel of mine that I rather like.)

But sadly, Hubin is doing other things now, and the position is currently held by a truly incompetent reviewer named Marilyn Stasio. During the last Mystery Writers of America award celebration—where authors sit on panels and talk to the audience—Stasio held court, allowing writers to present themselves to her and do a little recreational bowing and scraping. As one editor told me: "It was one of the most nauseating things I've ever seen. This woman is a joke, yet here were all these very accomplished writers fawning over her."

But don't ask *me* about Marilyn Stasio. Ask Charles Grodin. He did a fine angry number on her on his talk show recently. I mention the Stasio incident because I think most of us give influential reviewers far more importance than they deserve.

Obviously, critics aren't going to go away. They build up followings and thus become sources of revenue for their magazines. And some critics *do* write well, are frequently entertaining, and actually have something serious to say about craft.

My third novel did well by some critics, badly by others. The most valuable review for me, however, was a mixed one I received in a major midwestern paper. The reviewer liked the characters and the story but was not at all happy with how I handled place description and set scenes. And you know what? He was correct. I did an amateurish job with these aspects of the book. I called him and thanked him for making those particular points, and I still remember what he said: "I can't believe it. A writer *thanking* me for taking shots at his book." We both had a good laugh.

Constructive criticism, I guess you'd call it. The man made a better writer out of me and I was properly grateful. He wasn't trying to impress his readers with his wit or erudition, he was just honestly assessing my novel as he saw it.

IV

You're going to have a great time with this book. You're going to start calling people and reading them some of the best quotes. And the next time you have friends over, you'll probably drag the book out and start quoting it at length. Hell, you may even have a *Critics Were Wrong!* party.

What goes around comes around.

That's what this book is all about: a little vengeance on behalf of writers, directors, actors, composers, and producers everywhere.

Enjoy.

—Ed Gorman*

Publisher's Weekly called Ed Gorman's most recent suspense novel, *Blood Moon*, "An expertly wrought atmospheric mystery" while *Kirkus Reviews* called his mainstream novel, *The Marilyn Tapes*, "Deliciously slick." Of Gorman generally, Britain's *Million* noted: "John D. MacDonald meets Jim Thompson....Gorman is one of the world's great storytellers."

On the other hand, Gorman has also been called a "literary sociopath," a "pornographer," and a "writer of dark, edgy, and frequently depressing thrillers."

He feels right at home with many of the reviews in this book. He's gotten some even worse ones himself.

The Critics Were
Wrong ————————————

1

Maligned Masterpieces

The Great Films and the Critics Who Missed It

Adam's Rib
1949

> DIRECTOR: George Cukor; SCREENPLAY: Ruth Gordon,
> Garson Kanin; CAST: Spencer Tracy, Katharine Hepburn,
> David Wayne, Tom Ewell, Judy Holliday.
> Selected to the National Film Registry, Library of
> Congress. Academy Award nomination for Best Screenplay.

"The balance of the picture, which observes the Tracy-Hepburns at home, is plain embarrassing." —Robert Hatch, *New Republic,* January 9, 1950

"Where the principals are concerned, the humor is often crudely risqué, the antics forced and embarrassingly coy, the lines inane. A sophisticated effort that turns out mainly *silly.*" —Jane Lockhart, *Rotarian,* February, 1950

The Adventures of Robin Hood
1938

> DIRECTOR: William Keighley, Michael Curtiz; SCREENPLAY:
> Seton I. Miller, Norman Reilly Raine; CAST: Errol Flynn,

Basil Rathbone, Claude Rains, Olivia de Havilland, Alan
Hale.

Academy Award winner for Best Score, Art Direction,
Editing; nomination for Best Picture.

"...what I would like to question is not whether this is a
good picture, of which there is no doubt it isn't, but
whether those who get their first idea of Robin Hood
from its pitilessly graphic statement can ever dissociate
the ideal from the sad mechanics of its film production,
because in direction and purpose this *Robin Hood* is
focused in the character of Errol Flynn, a hard and agile
worker. I wonder who would ever be truly inspired by a
People's Defender as smooth of contour, endless of
resilience, and full of human feeling as an inner
tube." —Otis Ferguson, *New Republic,* June 8, 1938

The African Queen
1952

DIRECTOR: John Huston; SCREENPLAY: James Agee; CAST:
Humphrey Bogart, Katharine Hepburn, Robert Morley,
Peter Bull.

Academy Award winner for Best Actor; nominations for
Best Screenplay, Director, Actress.

"...the yarn won't wash...you cross your legs in irrita-
tion and wish yourself home with Jules Verne. For one
thing, the picture does not move fast enough to outstrip
your doubts; for another Agee and John Huston, the
director, have made the mistake of injecting notes of
realistic personality into their characters, for a third, the
expense of all this foolishness is oppressively evi-
dent." —Robert Hatch, *New Republic,* March 10, 1952

L'Age d'Or
1930

DIRECTOR: Luis Buñuel; SCREENPLAY: Luis Buñuel, Salvador Dali; CAST: Gaston Modot, Lya Lys, Max Ernst, Pierre Prévert, Jacques Brunius.

"The written synopsis is much more entertaining than the picture, which is a pretentious bore. If the Film Society would like to see Ideology in mature yet convincing and healthy form, I suggest they take a look at a Silly Symphony called *Spring Song,* and another Walt Disney picture, Mickey Mouse's performance of *Uncle Tom's Cabin.*" —Pare Lorentz, *Vanity Fair,* May 1933

Alexander Nevsky
1938

DIRECTOR: Sergei Eisenstein; SCREENPLAY: Pyotr Pavlenko, Sergei Eisenstein; CAST: Nikolai Cherkassov, Nikolai Okhlopkov, Andrei Abrikossov.

"Each attitude, point, and symbol hangs on like a drowning man...and if the best close-up you can get of a knight on horseback is by putting a man in a rocking chair with a champagne bucket over his head, you would do best to skip the close-up....Far from being the thumping great film people come to expect of a thumping name, *Alexander Nevsky* is way behind the good Soviet (and how many other) films of the last five years, in conception, story, pace, and vital meaning." —Otis Ferguson, *New Republic,* April 12, 1939

All About Eve
1950

DIRECTOR: Joseph L. Mankiewicz; SCREENPLAY: Joseph L. Mankiewicz; CAST: Bette Davis, George Sanders, Anne Baxter, Celeste Holm, Thelma Ritter.

Selected to the National Film Registry, Library of Congress. Academy Award winner for Best Picture, Director, Screenplay, Actor; nominations for Cinematography, Score, Actress, Supporting Actress, Art Direction, Editing.

"...the bitchiest fabrication since Mrs. Luce's *The Women*. It is not true, as you may have heard, that *All About Eve* is a great picture and proof that Hollywood has grown up overnight. Its highly polished, often witty surface hides an unenterprising plot and some preposterous human behavior." —Robert Hatch, *New Republic*, November 6, 1950

An American in Paris
1951

DIRECTOR: Vincente Minnelli; SCREENPLAY: Alan Jay Lerner; CAST: Gene Kelly, Oscar Levant, Nina Foch, Leslie Caron.

Selected to the National Film Registry, Library of Congress. Academy Award winner for Best Picture, Screenplay, Cinematography, Musical Arrangements, Art Direction; nominations for Director, Editing.

"The publicity led this reviewer to expect something unusual...But this is substantially the same old stuff. It used to be set in Mexico and used to star Xavier Cugat and a chihuahua." —William Pfaff, *Commonweal*, October 19, 1951

Leslie Caron and Gene Kelly in *An American in Paris*

"...completely pointless choreography written and executed by the insistently masculine Gene Kelly...It is certainly true that the movies can produce ballet effects impossible on a stage, but that these visual gymnastics are diverting enough to make form and wit and taste unnecessary remains to be proved. The rest of the picture...is crass. No excesses of stale cuteness are spared the cast by Vincente Minnelli in his desperate efforts to exact some animation from the spiritless script." —Robert Hatch, *New Republic,* October 22, 1951

Annie Hall
1977

DIRECTOR: Woody Allen; SCREENPLAY: Woody Allen, Marshall Brickman; CAST: Woody Allen, Diane Keaton, Tony Roberts, Carol Kane.

Selected to the National Film Registry, Library of Congress. Academy Award winner for Best Picture, Screenplay, Director, Actress; nomination for Best Actor. Winner of British Academy of Film and Television Arts awards for Film, Director, Actress, Screenplay; Directors Guild of America award, and Writers Guild of America, West award for Screenplay.

"With *Annie Hall,* Woody Allen has truly underreached himself...his new film is painful in three separate ways: as unfunny comedy, poor moviemaking, and embarrassing self-revelation. It is everything we never wanted to know about Woody's sex life and were afraid he'd tell us anyway. And now he does...It is a film so shapeless, sprawling, repetitious, and aimless as to seem to beg for oblivion." —John Simon, *New York,* May 2, 1977

Beauty and the Beast (*La Belle et la bête*) _____
1946

DIRECTOR: Jean Cocteau; SCREENPLAY: Jean Cocteau; CAST:
Jean Marais, Josette Day, Mila Parély, Marcel André.

"There is nothing wrong with the Beast in *Beauty and the Beast*...that a shave, a haircut, and a bit of bridgework wouldn't clear up just as effectively as the love of a handsome princess...I'd like to recommend *Beauty and the Beast* for children during this festive season, but I can't, since I fear it would give them the horrors...."
—John McCarten, *New Yorker*, December 20, 1947

"The beast is too repellent for any but the most unimpressionable children, and the film as a whole will confirm adults in their belief that they have outgrown fairy tales. The celebrated Cocteau imagination appears to have been drowsing through this production."
—Robert Hatch, *New Republic*, December 29, 1947

The Best Years of Our Lives _____
1946

DIRECTOR: William Wyler; SCREENPLAY: Robert Sherwood,
from the novel *Glory for Me*, by MacKinlay Kantor; CAST:
Fredric March, Myrna Loy, Teresa Wright, Dana Andrews,
Harold Russell.

Selected to the National Film Registry, Library of
Congress. Academy Award winner for Best Picture,
Screenplay, Director, Score, Actor, Supporting Actor,
Editing.

"It takes about three hours to run off *The Best Years of Our Lives*, which is the longest picture Samuel Goldwyn ever made. Before the drama has finally resolved itself, the spectator is inclined to suspect that he's watching the longest picture *anybody* ever made....Considering the fact that Mr. Goldwyn spent three million dollars on it and hired Robert E. Sherwood to beat it into shape out of four hundred and thirty-four pages of blank verse by MacKinlay Kantor, he had every right to expect something better than this." —John McCarten, *New Yorker,* November 23, 1946

The Big Sleep
1946

DIRECTOR: Howard Hawks; SCREENPLAY: William Faulkner, Leigh Brackett, Jules Furthman, from the novel by Raymond Chandler; CAST: Humphrey Bogart, Lauren Bacall, John Ridgely, Martha Vickers, Dorothy Malone, Regis Toomey, Charles Waldron.

"If somebody had only told us—the script-writers, preferably—just what it is that happens in the Warners' and Howard Hawks' *The Big Sleep,* we might be able to give you a more explicit and favorable report on this over-age melodrama....the whole thing comes off a poisonous picture lasting a few minutes shy of two hours..." —Bosley Crowther, *New York Times,* April 24, 1946

The Birth of a Nation
1915

DIRECTOR: D. W. Griffith; SCREENPLAY: D. W. Griffith, Frank E. Woods; CAST: Henry B. Walthall, Mae Marsh, Miriam Cooper, Lillian Gish.

Selected to the National Film Registry, Library of Congress. Voted the best silent film in a 1971 *Daily Variety* poll of 200 filmmakers.

"Whatever happened during Reconstruction, this film is aggressively vicious and defamatory. It is spiritual assassination. It degrades the censors that passed it and the white race that endures it." —Francis Hackett, *New Republic*, March 20, 1915

Bonnie and Clyde
1967

DIRECTOR: Arthur Penn; SCREENPLAY: David Newman, Robert Benton; CAST: Warren Beatty, Faye Dunaway, Gene Hackman, Estelle Parsons, Michael J. Pollard.

Selected to the National Film Registry, Library of Congress. Academy Award winner for Cinematography, Best Supporting Actress; nominations for Best Picture, Screenplay, Director, Actor, Actress, Supporting Actor. Winner of the New York Film Critics Circle award for Best Screenplay and the Laurel Screen Award for Drama presented by the Writers Guild of America, West.

"Producer Beatty and Director Arthur Penn have elected to tell their tale of bullets and blood in a strange and purposeless mingling of fact and claptrap that teeters uneasily on the brink of burlesque. Like Bonnie and Clyde themselves, the film rides off in all directions and ends up full of holes." —*Time*, August 25, 1967

"Conceptually, the film leaves much to be desired, because killings and the backdrop of the depression are scarcely material for a bundle of laughs.... Characterizations are, in the main, inconsistent and confusing." —*Variety*, August 9, 1967

Poster for *The Bride of Frankenstein*

The Bride of Frankenstein ───────────────
1935

DIRECTOR: James Whale; SCREENPLAY: John L. Balderston, William Hurlbut; CAST: Boris Karloff, Colin Clive, Ernest Thesiger, Elsa Lanchester.

"This is not Mrs. Shelley's dream, but the dream of a committee of film executives who wanted to go one better than Mrs. Shelley and let Frankenstein create a second monster from the churchyard refuse, a woman this time, forgetting that the horror of the first creation is quite lost when it is repeated, and that the breeding of

monsters can become no more exciting than the breeding of poultry....This is a pompous, badly acted film, full of absurd anachronisms and inconsistencies."
—Graham Greene, *Spectator,* July 5, 1935

Casablanca
1942

> DIRECTOR: Michael Curtiz; SCREENPLAY: Julius J. Epstein, Philip G. Epstein, Howard Koch; CAST: Humphrey Bogart, Ingrid Bergman, Paul Henreid, Claude Rains, Sydney Greenstreet, Peter Lorre, S. Z. Sakall, Conrad Veidt, Dooley Wilson.

Sydney Greenstreet and Humphrey Bogart in
Casablanca. The Maltese Falcon **was to come later.**

Selected to the National Film Registry, Library of Congress. Academy Award winner for Best Picture, Screenplay, Director; nominations for Cinematography, Best Score, Actor, Supporting Actor (Claude Rains), Editing.

"Hollywood often uses its best players, writers and directors for its epic phonies.... Each studio has its preference.... Warner's is *Casablanca*... The *Casablanca* kind of hokum was good in its original context in other movies, but, lifted into *Casablanca* for the sake of its glitter and not incorporated into it, loses its meaning.... Bogart's humanitarian killer, who was disillusioned apparently at his mother's breast, has to say some silly things and to play God too often to be as believably tough as he was in his last eight pictures." —Manny Farber, *New Republic*, December 14, 1942

Children of Paradise (*Les Enfants du paradis*) _____
1945

DIRECTOR: Marcel Carné; SCREENPLAY: Jacques Prévert; CAST: Arletty, Jean-Louis Barrault, Pierre Brasseur.

Academy Award nomination for Best Screenplay.

"The most ambitious French film, and certainly the longest, to cross the Atlantic since the Nazis were pushed back of the Seine, turns out to be a strange mixture of the beautiful, the esoteric and the downright dull..." —*Variety*, February 26, 1947

"Whenever the action shows a tendency to flag, M. Prévert breaks out a fiesta, and if you are as intolerant of fiestas as I am, I don't think you're going to have much fun sitting through the noise and confusion...altogether it's much closer to middling fare than you'd expect..." —John McCarten, *New Yorker*, February 15, 1947

Chinatown
1974

DIRECTOR: Roman Polanski; SCREENPLAY: Robert Towne;
CAST: Jack Nicholson, Faye Dunaway, John Huston.
Selected to the National Film Registry, Library of
Congress. Academy Award winner for Best Screenplay;
nominations for Best Picture, Director, Cinematography,
Score, Actor, Actress. British Academy of Film and
Television Arts award for Actor, Director, Screenplay;
Golden Globe winner for Actor, Director, Picture,
Screenplay; New York Film Critics Circle award for Best
Actor; Writers Guild of America, West award winner for
Screenplay.

"The formulation Polanski wants to make between the
dregs of society and the cream might have inspired a
good movie. But *Chinatown* isn't it.... The whole movie is
an attempt both to hint that Polanski is still a serious,
original stylist and to make a commercial hit no matter
how derivative and trendy." —Colin L. Westerbeck Jr.,
Commonweal, July 26, 1974

A Christmas Carol
1951

DIRECTOR: Brian Desmond Hurst; SCREENPLAY: Noel
Langley, from the story by Charles Dickens; CAST: Alastair
Sim, Kathleen Harrison, Jack Warner, Michael Hordern,
Mervyn Johns, Hermione Baddeley.

"It is a grim thing that will give tender-aged kiddies
viewing it the screaming meemies, and adults will find it
long, dull and greatly overdone.... Alastair Sim, without
directorial or script restraint, stalks through the footage
like a tanktown Hamlet, and the other players do no
better.... Ghostly visitations and Sim's reaction to them,

particularly the initial shade, are ludicrous in the extreme but with still enough horror to scare the kiddies nearly to death." —*Variety*, November 14, 1951

David Copperfield
1934

DIRECTOR: George Cukor; SCREENPLAY: Hugh Walpole, Howard Estabrook, from the novel by Charles Dickens; CAST: Freddie Bartholomew, Frank Lawton, W. C. Fields, Roland Young, Edna May Oliver, Lennox Pawle, Basil Rathbone, Violet Kemble Cooper, Maureen O'Sullivan, Lionel Barrymore, Herbert Mundin.

Academy Award nominations for Best Picture, Editing.

"It would be unnecessarily dull to enlarge on the reasons why the version of *David Copperfield* at the Capitol is not, and could not be, altogether satisfactory entertainment....George Cukor has had the good sense to let the long roll of familiar characters parade before the eye with such rapidity that no interruption of the mind is possible. The direction, unmarked by any originality or striking quality of style, is exactly right for the intention." —William Troy, *Nation*, February 6, 1935

The Day the Earth Stood Still
1951

DIRECTOR: Robert Wise; SCREENPLAY: Edmund H. North; CAST: Michael Rennie, Patricia Neal, Hugh Marlowe, Sam Jaffe.

"Don't be alarmed, we confidently tell you, because, once this contraption is down and its pilots have emerged from its innards on the ellipse in Washington, they turn out to be such decent fellows, so well-mannered and

peacefully inclined, that you'd hardly expect them to
split an infinitive, let alone an atom or a human
head.... We've seen better monsters in theatre audiences
on 42d Street." —Bosley Crowther, *New York Times*,
September 19, 1951

"...the director, Mr. Robert Wise, and the script are
entirely unequal to working out the situation they have
presented...the film would be infinitely more entertaining if the imagination of those responsible for it had
even tried to challenge the implications of their
theme..." —*London Times*, December 14, 1951

The Discreet Charm of the Bourgeoisie _____
1972

DIRECTOR: Luis Buñuel; SCREENPLAY: Luis Buñuel, Jean-
Claude Carrière; CAST: Fernando Rey, Delphine Seyrig,
Stéphane Audran.

Academy Award winner for Best Foreign Film;
nomination for Best Screenplay.

"Here is a film that has received rave notices from all
reviewers, top to bottom, and is doing well with local
audiences; yet I consider it absolutely worthless.... This
latest Buñuel film is a haphazard concatenation of waking and dream sequences in which anything goes, and
which would make just as much, or just as little, sense if
they were put together in any other disorder." —John
Simon, from his collection *Something to Declare*, 1983.

Dr. Strangelove or: How I Learned to Stop
Worrying and Love the Bomb _____
1963

DIRECTOR: Stanley Kubrick; SCREENPLAY: Stanley Kubrick,
Terry Southern, Peter George, from his book *Two Hours to*

Doom; CAST: Peter Sellers, George C. Scott, Sterling Hayden, Keenan Wynn, Slim Pickens, Peter Bull, James Earl Jones.

Selected to the National Film Registry, Library of Congress. Academy Award nominations for Best Picture, Screenplay, Director, Actor; British Academy of Film and Television Arts award for Best Film; Writers Guild of America, West award for Best Comedy.

"...often his jokes are on the childish level of risque skits in a cheap burlesque show...he mixes bright satirical wit with slapstick, pointless wisecracks about sex, and phallic symbols that even a beginning psychology student would consider puerile...While a few of the critics are now calling Stanley Kubrick a 'boy genius,' I'm wondering if the emphasis shouldn't be more on 'boy' and less on 'genius.'" —Philip T. Hartung, *Commonweal*, February 21, 1964

"...twirpish twiddle..." —H. H., *Films in Review*, February 1964

"Stanley Kubrick's new film...is beyond any question the most shattering sick joke I've ever come across....The ultimate touch of goulish humor is when we see the bomb actually going off, dropped on some point in Russia, and a jazzy sound track comes in with a cheerful melodic rendition of "We'll Meet Again Some Sunny Day." Somehow, to me, it isn't funny. It is malefic and sick." —Bosley Crowther, *New York Times*, January 31, 1964

La Dolce Vita
1960

DIRECTOR: Federico Fellini; SCREENPLAY: Federico Fellini, Tullio Pinelli, Ennio Flaiano, Brunello Rondi; CAST: Marcello Mastroianni, Anita Ekberg, Anouk Aimée.

Academy Award nominations for Best Screenplay,
Director; Palme d'Or award at Cannes Film Festival.

"Federico Fellini's new film is a three-hour peep-show—
a carelessly written and directed hodge-podge of skits
depicting some of the follies of contemporary Western
civilization....Those critics who regard it as a moral
indictment of decadence seem to me to be over-kind. It is
too unintegrated, and too ambiguous, to merit consider-
ation of so serious a sort. At bottom, and in the language
of the trade, it is an 'exploitation' picture, i.e., a movie
which can be promoted so as to attract sensation-
seekers....There is no noteworthy acting." —Henry
Hart, *Films in Review,* June/July 1961

Double Indemnity
1944

DIRECTOR: Billy Wilder; SCREENPLAY: Billy Wilder, Raymond
Chandler, from the novel by James M. Cain; CAST: Fred
MacMurray, Barbara Stanwyck, Edward G. Robinson.
Selected to the National Film Registry, Library of
Congress.

"...the very toughness of the picture is also the weakness
of its core, and the academic nature of its plotting limits
its general appeal...The principal characters—an insur-
ance salesman and a wicked woman, which Mr. MacMurray
and Miss Stanwyck play—lack the attractiveness to ren-
der their fate of emotional consequences....Mr. Robinson is the only one you care two hoots for in the film.
The rest are just neatly carved pieces in a variably
intriguing crime game." —Bosley Crowther, *New York
Times,* September 7, 1944

8½

1963

DIRECTOR: Federico Fellini; SCREENPLAY: Federico Fellini,
Ennio Flaiano, Tullio Pinelli, Brunello Rondi; CAST: Marcello
Mastroianni, Claudia Cardinale, Anouk Aimée.

Academy Award winner for Best Foreign Film;
nominations for Best Director, Screenplay.

"…Apparently aware that his vogue cannot be sup-
ported much longer by such slender equipment, even

The puzzled director: Marcello Mastroianni in *8½*

allowing for the currently addled condition of Europe's intellectuals, Fellini has, in the melange he has called *8¹/₂*, undertaken to bid for sympathy by commenting upon himself, and his cinematic racketeering.... The result is more Fellini jumble—incidents of fact, dream, fantasy, and imagination strung together without reason and without art.... In their totality they mean nothing." —Helen Weldon Kuhn, *Fil ms in Review,* August/September 1963

Fanny and Alexander
1982

DIRECTOR: Ingmar Bergman; SCREENPLAY: Ingmar Bergman; CAST: Gunn Walgren, Ewa Fröling, Jarl Kulle, Erland Josephson.

Academy Award winner for Best Foreign Language Film, Cinematography, Art Direction; nominations for Director, Screenplay; Golden Globe winner for Best Foreign Film.

"Never an admirer to begin with, I think the latest film epitomizes his wildly overrated career. Even his fans will find it disappointing.... The failure of Bergman's vision is so total in *Fanny and Alexander* that the bad acting ultimately makes little difference. No more damning criticism could be made of a director who will be remembered, I believe, for nothing more (and nothing less) than having elsewhere elicited so many splendid performances." —Robert Asahina, *New Leader,* August 8 & 22, 1983

"I don't believe one word of this 'love' glup that runs from one end of the film to the other. When Ingmar Bergman talked to me of God and death I respected him despite his past political sympathies. But now that he's

•

prattling on about love, and gentle smiles, and fruit trees in bloom, I think something in him has snapped."
—Richard Grenier, *Commentary,* September 1983

"Few things are sadder than the attempt of a great artist, hitherto fully appreciated only by a minority, to reach the masses....There is nothing here that Bergman hasn't done better before, and we get bored....*Fanny and Alexander* is an overstuffed film, and, in this case at least, more is decidedly less." —John Simon, *National Review,* July 22, 1983

Fantasia
1940

> DIRECTOR: Ben Sharpsteen, Joe Grant, Dick Heumer;
> MUSICAL DIRECTOR: Leopold Stokowski.
>
> Selected to the National Film Registry, Library of Congress.

"A promising monstrosity...The essentially new and essentially problematic in *Fantasia* is the use of great music as accompaniment for Walt Disney cartoons. To be sure we are told that it is the other way around, and no doubt the intent was the opposite one, but the effects achieved are nevertheless Walt Disney plus Bach or Beethoven....to have the *Pastoral Symphony* interrupted by applause for sugar-sweet centaurettes is painful..."
—Franz Hoellering, *Nation,* November 23, 1940

"I left the theater in a condition bordering on nervous breakdown....I had no desire to throw myself in adoration before [those] responsible for the brutalization of sensibility in this remarkable nightmare." —Dorothy Thompson, *New York Herald Tribune,* November 14, 1940

Frankenstein
1931

DIRECTOR: James Whale; SCREENPLAY: Garrett Fort, Francis Edward Faragoh, John L. Balderston, from the novel by Mary Shelley; CAST: Boris Karloff, Colin Clive, Mae Clarke.

Selected to the National Film Registry, Library of Congress.

"Despite the advance publicity which advised me that 'to have seen *Frankenstein* is to wear a badge of courage'... I regret to report that it is just another movie, so thoroughly mixed with water as to have a horror content of about .0001 percent.... The film differs greatly from the book and soon turns into a sort of comic opera with a range of cardboard mountains over which extras in French Revolution costumes dash about with flaming torches." —Creighton Peet, *Outlook & Independent,* December 9, 1931

The General
1926

DIRECTOR: Buster Keaton, Clyde Bruckman; SCREENPLAY: Buster Keaton, Clyde Bruckman; CAST: Buster Keaton, Glenn Cavender, Jim Farley, Frederick Vroom, Marian Mack.

Selected to the National Film Registry, Library of Congress.

"Someone should have told Buster that it is difficult to derive laughter from the sight of men being killed in battle. Many of his gags at the end of the picture are in such gruesomely bad taste that the sympathetic spectator is inclined to look the other way." —Robert E. Sherwood, *Life,* February 24, 1927

"*The General* is far from funny. Its principal comedy scene is built on that elementary bit, the chase, and you can't continue a flight for almost an hour and expect results. Especially is this so when the action is placed entirely in the hands of the star. It was his story, he directed, and he acted. The result is a flop." —*Variety*, February 9, 1927

The Godfather Part II ———————————————
1974

DIRECTOR: Francis Ford Coppola; SCREENPLAY: Francis Ford Coppola, Mario Puzo, from his novel *The Godfather*; CAST: Al Pacino, Robert Duvall, Diane Keaton, Robert De Niro.

Selected to the National Film Registry, Library of Congress. Academy Award winner for Art Direction, Picture, Screenplay (Adapted), Director, Score, Supporting Actor; nominations for Actor, Supporting Actor, Supporting Actress. Winner of the British Academy of Film and Television Arts award for Best Actor, Directors Guild of America award and the Writers Guild of America, West award for Drama Adapted from Another Medium.

"It's a Frankenstein's monster stitched together from leftover parts. It talks. It moves in fits and starts but it has no mind of its own.... Everything of any interest was thoroughly covered in the original film, but like many people who have nothing to say, *Part II* won't shut up.... Looking very expensive but spiritually desperate, *Part II* has the air of a very long, very elaborate revue sketch." —Vincent Canby, *New York Times*, December 13, 1974

Gone With the Wind
1939

DIRECTOR: Victor Fleming; SCREENPLAY: Sidney Howard and others, from the novel by Margaret Mitchell; CAST: Clark Gable, Vivien Leigh, Olivia de Havilland, Leslie Howard, Thomas Mitchell, Hattie McDaniel, Butterfly McQueen. Selected to the National Film Registry, Library of Congress. Academy Award winner for Best Picture, Screenplay, Director, Cinematography, Actress, Supporting Actress, Film Editing, Art Direction; nominations for Score, Actor, Supporting Actress, Special Effects.

"It moves, just as I suspected it would, and it is in color, just as I heard it was, and the Civil War gets very civil indeed and there is a wonderful bonfire and there are also young love and balls and plantations and practically everything.... They threw in many good things, and everything else but a towel, and they got them in line and added them all up to one of the world's imposing cancellations." —Otis Ferguson, *New Republic*, April 22, 1940

"...will probably surge to success on the strength of its 'bestseller' story, on the strength of its stars, Vivien Leigh, Clark Gable, and Leslie Howard (who perform the required gestures competently), and even—such are our present discontents—on the strength of its length. But none of that will ever make it a good film, any more than the Bearded Lady in a circus sideshow can ever be quite the same attraction as the pure and satisfactory sawdust circle of the Big Tent itself." —Basil Wright, *Spectator*, April 26, 1940

"...a major disappointment..." —Allen Bishop, *Theatre Arts*, February 1940

Gunga Din
1939

DIRECTOR: George Stevens; SCREENPLAY: Joel Sayre, Fred
Guiol, Ben Hecht, Charles MacArthur from the poem by
Rudyard Kipling; CAST: Cary Grant, Victor McLaglen,
Douglas Fairbanks Jr., Sam Jaffe.

"The fighting has terrific motion, the elephant is fine,
the battalion parade with bagpipes is always good for a
lift, and the only thing lacking from the temple rites is
Bela Lugosi. But the fact is that they can neither believe
their own hokum nor leave it alone.... It is not so much
that they'll stop at nothing here as that they'll start with
nothing and keep on till it bleeds." —Otis Ferguson,
New Republic, February 22, 1939

High Noon
1952

DIRECTOR: Fred Zinnemann; SCREENPLAY: Carl Foreman;
CAST: Gary Cooper, Grace Kelly, Thomas Mitchell.

Selected to the National Film Registry, Library of
Congress. Academy Award winner for Best Actor, Score,
Title Song, Editing; nominations for Best Picture,
Screenplay, Director.

"A deftly fouled-up Western...someone spent too much
time over the drawing board conceiving dramatic camera shots to cover up the lack of story. Moral: the Kramer
gang (*Champion, The Men*) is making too many films for
its own good." —Manny Farber, *Nation*, April 26, 1952

"...regrettable in its implication that violence is the only
way out, the only standard worth upholding."
—*Christian Century*, September 10, 1952

Intolerance ————————————————————
1916

DIRECTOR: D. W. Griffith; SCREENPLAY: D. W. Griffith; CAST:
Mae Marsh, Lillian Gish, Constance Talmadge, Robert
Harron, Elmo Lincoln, Eugene Pallette.
   Selected to the National Film Registry, Library of
Congress.

"...The attempt is not to stimulate the imagination, but
to gorge the senses. Even this attempt is unsuccessful,
because the illusion is not played for honestly; one is
astounded at the tricks, the expense, the machinery of
production, more often than one is absorbed by their
result. One might enjoy a quarter of it, stretched out to
the full time. But as it is, one prefers Messrs. Barnum
and Bailey." —George Soule, *New Republic*, September
30, 1916

It's a Wonderful Life ————————————————
1946

DIRECTOR: Frank Capra; SCREENPLAY: Frances Goodrich,
Albert Hackett, Frank Capra; CAST: James Stewart, Henry
Travers, Donna Reed, Lionel Barrymore.
   Selected to the National Film Registry, Library of
Congress. Academy Award nominations for Best Picture,
Director, Actor, Editing.

"...the latest example of Capracorn, shows his art at a
hysterical pitch..." —Manny Farber, *New Republic*,
January 6, 1947

"...Mr. Capra has seen to it that practically all the actors
involved behave as cutely as pixies. I suppose it's all
meant to show that there's nothing like a real American

boy for bringing out the good in the worst of us—
perhaps a sound proposition but hardly one that im-
proves by being enunciated in terms so mincing as to
border on baby talk." —John McCarten, *New Yorker,*
December 21, 1946

Jules and Jim
1962

> DIRECTOR: François Truffaut; SCREENPLAY: François Truffaut,
> Jean Gruault; CAST: Oskar Werner, Jeanne Moreau, Henri
> Serre.

"New Waver Truffaut is playing an old game. *Jules and Jim*
is that ponderous old party, the message movie—tricked
up with fleeting close-ups, stopped motion and sudden
cuts.... The more films by young French directors that
come to this country, the harder it gets to be enchanted by
the sight of adults skipping across hill, and fields."
—*Newsweek,* May 7, 1962

Last Year at Marienbad
1961

> DIRECTOR: Alain Resnais; SCREENPLAY: Alain Robbe-Grillet;
> CAST: Delphine Seyrig, Giorgio Albertazzi, Sacha Pitoeff.
> Academy Award nominations for Best Story and Screenplay.

"I got one clear impression from *Last Year at Marienbad,*
and that was of Resnais and Robbe-Grillet grinning
wickedly at each other above the heads of a trustful
public that was flagging its poor little brain into some

notion of what in hell the picture is all about."
—Robert Hatch, *Nation,* March 24, 1962

"*Marienbad* is unassailable and unarguable, because it has been deliberately made to mean all things to all men.... Resnais has created a spectacle that is elaborate, ponderous, and meaningless." —*Newsweek,* March 19, 1962

"The simple truth about *Last Year at Marienbad* is that a not untalented young filmaker (Resnais) has forsworn the hard work artistic creation entails, and has allowed his immature and meaningless fumbling to be promoted by those who wish to convert Western culture into an irrational confusion." —Louise Corbin, *Films in Review,* April 1962

Laura
1944

DIRECTOR: Otto Preminger; SCREENPLAY: Jay Dratler, Samuel Hoffenstein, Betty Reinhardt from the novel by Vera Caspary; CAST: Dana Andrews, Clifton Webb, Gene Tierney.

Academy Award winner for Cinematography; nominations for Best Screenplay, Director, Supporting Actor, Art Direction.

"As a murder puzzle it leaves out most of the clues and hides the rest, which makes the mystery both baffling and boring...it is hard to find anything good in *Laura,* or simply anything." —Manny Farber, *New Republic,* October 30, 1944

Lawrence of Arabia _____
1962

DIRECTOR: David Lean; SCREENPLAY: Robert Bolt; CAST: Peter
O'Toole, Alec Guinness, Anthony Quinn, Jack Hawkins, Jose
Ferrer, Anthony Quayle, Claude Rains, Arthur Kennedy,
Donald Wolfit, Omar Sharif.

Selected to the National Film Registry, Library of
Congress. Academy Award winner for Best Picture, Director,
Score, Cinematography, Film Editing; nominations for
Actor, Supporting Actor, Screenplay. Winner of British
Academy of Film and Television Arts awards for Film,
Actor, Screenplay. Golden Globe awards for Picture,
Director, Supporting Actor, Cinematography.

"It is, in the last analysis, just a huge, thundering camel-
opera that tends to run down rather badly as it rolls on
into its third hour and gets involved with sullen disillu-
sion and political deceit." —Bosley Crowther, *New York
Times*, December 17, 1962

"...a galumphing camelodrama in *debut de siecle*
style...Indeed the acting, dialogue, and direction are all
so uniformly elephantine one feels that the film can't
have been directed in the usual sense at all. It seems to
have been 'panavisualized' instead...compounded by an
unspeakably turgid score it was a relief to hear now and
then an eruptive camel-grunt." —Roger Sandall, *Film
Quarterly*, Spring 1963

"Simply another expensive mirage, dull, overlong, and
coldly impersonal...on the whole I find it hatefully
calculating and condescending...If a beautiful girl were
stripped and then flogged for her resistence, the censors
would be up in arms demanding an end to this immoral-
ity...but let a man be stripped and flogged, and we are

Omar Sharif, Peter O'Toole, and Anthony Quinn in
Lawrence of Arabia

supposed to be impressed with the seriousness of the
theme. Perhaps *Lawrence of Arabia* is one brutal queer
film too many..." —Andrew Sarris, *Village Voice*,
December 20, 1962

The Magnificent Ambersons
1942

> DIRECTOR: Orson Welles; SCREENPLAY: Orson Welles, from
> the novel by Booth Tarkington; CAST: Joseph Cotten,
> Dolores Costello, Agnes Moorehead, Tim Holt.
>
> Selected to the National Film Registry, Library of
> Congress. Academy Award nominations for Best Picture,
> Cinematography, Supporting Actress.

"Orson Welles's second I-did-it should show once and for all that film making, radio and the stage are three different guys better kept separated...While telling this story, haltingly and clumsily, the movie runs from burdensome through heavy and dull to bad. It stutters and stumbles as Welles submerges Tarkington's story in a mess of radio and stage technique...Aside from all the dead spots the story is told as badly as would seem possible. —Manny Farber, *New Republic,* August 10, 1942

Mr. Smith Goes to Washington _____
1939

DIRECTOR: Frank Capra; SCREENPLAY: Sidney Buchman; CAST: James Stewart, Claude Rains, Jean Arthur.

Selected to the National Film Registry, Library of Congress. Academy Award winner for Best Original Story; nominations for Best Picture, Screenplay, Director, Score, Actor, Supporting Actor, Art Direction.

"*Mr. Smith Goes to Washington* is going to be the big movie explosion of the year, and reviewers are going to think twice and think sourly before they'll want to put it down for the clumsy and irritating thing it is....Politically, the story is eyewash....one scout leader who knows the Gettysburg address by heart but wouldn't possibly be hired to mow your lawn can throw passionate faith into the balance and by God we've got a fine free country to live in again." —Otis Ferguson, *New Republic,* November 1, 1939

Modern Times
1936

DIRECTOR: Charles Chaplin; SCREENPLAY: Charles Chaplin;
CAST: Charles Chaplin, Paulette Goddard, Henry Bergman,
Chester Conklin, Tiny Sandford.

Selected to the National Film Registry, Library of
Congress.

"Chaplin was always a master of pathos. But pathos
seems to have overtaken him at last. The title of his new
satirical farce is pathetic.... It was slow in the making,
late to appear, and now, dear me, it's ten years behind the
times." —John Marks, *New Statesman*, February 15, 1936

Poster for *Modern Times*

Morocco ───────────────────────────
1930

DIRECTOR: Josef Von Sternberg; SCREENPLAY: Jules
Furthman; CAST: Marlene Dietrich, Gary Cooper, Adolphe
Menjou.
  Selected to the National Film Registry, Library of
Congress. Academy Award nominations for Best Director,
Cinematography, Actress, Art Direction.

"...ridiculous as a story, devoid of interesting characters,
and not very pretty as photography..."   —*New
Statesman and Nation,* April 4, 1931

My Darling Clementine ──────────────
1946

DIRECTOR: John Ford; SCREENPLAY: Samuel G. Engel,
Winston Miller; CAST: Henry Fonda, Victor Mature, Walter
Brennan.
  Selected to the National Film Registry, Library of
Congress.

"John Ford's slow-poke cowboy epic *My Darling Clementine*
is a dazzling example of how to ruin some wonderful
Western history with pompous movie making. Made
almost unrecognizable by this super-schmaltzing by 20th
Century-Fox, this is an account of how Wyatt Earp
(Henry Fonda) and his brothers rode herd on the bad-
men in Tombstone. Given almost equal billing with the
Earps in this version of old Tombstone are cloudscapes
which are as saccharine as postcard art. Typical of
director Ford's unimaginative, conforming tourist sensibility is the setting he uses."   —Manny Farber, *New
Republic,* December 16, 1946

Night of the Hunter ────────────────────────
1955

DIRECTOR: Charles Laughton; SCREENPLAY: James Agee;
CAST: Robert Mitchum, Shelley Winters, Lillian Gish, Billy
Chapin, Sally Jane Bruce.
Selected to the National Film Registry, Library of
Congress.

"From the start, Laughton was defeated in his efforts to
infuse the materials with a significance at all comparable
to their distastefulness." —Moira Walsh, *America*,
October 8, 1955

"What *The Night of the Hunter* lacks most of all, in spite of
the good performances of Master Chapin and Miss Gish,
is heart. It's strong on Art, but has a cool contempt for
people." —Philip T. Hartung, *Commonweal*, October 7,
1955

The Nights of Cabiria (*La Notti di Cabiria*) ────────
1957

DIRECTOR: Federico Fellini; SCREENPLAY: Federico Fellini,
Ennio Flaiano, Tullio Pinelli; CAST: Giulietta Masina,
François Périer, Amedeo Nazzari.
Academy Award winner for Best Foreign Film. Cannes
Film Festival award for Best Actress.

"There are signs that some U.S. critics are no longer
taken in by the reclame manufactured in Europe for the
films Federico Fellini makes for box office purposes. Not
that *Cabiria* could be box office in the U.S. It is too
ineptly written and *directed,* and too synthetic.... As a
motion picture *Cabiria* is of no consequence, but so-
ciologically it could have utility as an illustration of how
sick Europe is." —L.C., *Films in Review*, December 1957

Nosferatu the Vampire ——————————————
1921

DIRECTOR: F. W. Murnau; SCREENPLAY: Henrik Galeen; CAST:
Max Schreck, Gustav Wangenheim, Alexander Granach.

"It is the sort of thing one could watch at midnight without
its having much effect upon one's slumbering
hours.... most of it seems like cardboard puppets doing
all they can to be horrible on papier-mache settings... It is
a production that is rather more of a soporific than a
thriller." —Mordaunt Hall, *New York Times,* June 4, 1929

Ordet ——————————————————————————
1957

DIRECTOR: Carl Theodor Dreyer; SCREENPLAY: Carl Theodor
Dreyer; CAST: Henrik Malberg, Emil Hass Christensen.
Golden Globe winner for Best Foreign Film.

"The background is so impressive that it takes the viewer
some time (maybe ten minutes) to realize that *Ordet* is a
turkey. It is pretentious, humorless, obscure, and the
nearest thing to immobility that the screen has thus far
achieved." —Robert Hatch, *Nation,* December 21, 1957

Paths of Glory ————————————————————
1957

DIRECTOR: Stanley Kubrick; SCREENPLAY: Stanley Kubrick,
Calder Willingham, Jim Thompson, from the novel by
Humphrey Cobb; CAST: Kirk Douglas, Adolphe Menjou,
George Macready.

Selected to the National Film Registry, Library of Congress.

"Those who have admired the motion picture work of this erstwhile still photographer will regret that in *Paths of Glory* camera angles seem to preoccupy him less than political ones, which, in view of the present state of the world, seem, to put it gently, immature and irresponsible. Kirk Douglas, whose own producing company is responsible for this tendentious film, plays Colonel Dax....His acting limitations are not obscured by Mr. Kubrick's direction." —Louise Bruce, *Films in Review*, January 1958

A Place in the Sun
1951

DIRECTOR: George Stevens; SCREENPLAY: Michael Wilson, Harry Brown, from the novel *An American Tragedy*, by Theodore Dreiser; CAST: Montgomery Clift, Elizabeth Taylor, Shelley Winters.

Selected to the National Film Registry, Library of Congress. Academy Award winner for Best Screenplay, Director, Cinematography, Score, Editing; nominations for Best Picture, Actor (Montgomery Clift), Supporting Actress (Shelley Winters).

"Unfortunately, the power and bite of the book have been lost in the polite competence of the screen. These are such nice, such obviously successful people, they must be playing charades....there doesn't seem much use in dragging Dreiser's classic off the shelf just to dress it in this elegant, ambivalent production..." —Robert Hatch, *New Republic*, September 10, 1951

The memorable scene on the steps of the Odessa
waterfront in *Potemkin*

Potemkin (also known as *The Battleship Potemkin*) — 1925

DIRECTOR: Sergei Eisenstein; SCREENPLAY: Sergei Eisenstein;
CAST: Alexander Antonov, Grigori Alexandrov, Vladimir
Barsky, Mikhail Goronorov.

Selected by a jury of 112 film historians from 26 countries
at the 1958 Brussels World's Fair as one of the Top Ten Best
Films of All Time.

"Those that are out-and-out reds, and those that are
inclined to socialism will undoubtedly find great things
about the picture, but hardly anyone else will.... To

Russians this may all mean something. As a pictorial historical record for the archives of the Soviet Government it may also mean something, but to the average American, unless he be an out-and-out red, it doesn't mean a damn. And that's that." —*Variety*, December 8, 1926

Psycho

1960

DIRECTOR: Alfred Hitchcock; SCREENPLAY: Joseph Stefano, from the novel by Robert Bloch; CAST: Anthony Perkins, Vera Miles, John Gavin, Janet Leigh.

Selected to the National Film Registry, Library of Congress. Academy Award nominations for Best Director, Cinematography, Supporting Actress, Art Direction.

"...one is confronted with a dilemma which can perhaps best be resolved by staying home. For this is third-rate Hitchcock, a Grand Guignol drama in which the customers hang around just for the tiny thrill at the end.... I think the film is a reflection of a most unpleasant mind, a mean, sly, sadistic little mind.... All in all, a nasty little film." —Dwight Macdonald, *Esquire,* October 1960

"...the director gets so far out that his chief sources of inspiration appear to have been Krafft-Ebing and the Marquis de Sade... Hitchcock seems to have been more interested in shocking his audience with the bloodiest bathtub murder in screen history, and in photographing Janet Leigh in various stages of undress, than in observing the ordinary rules of good film construction. This is a dangerous corner for a gifted movie maker to place himself in." —Moira Walsh, *America,* July 9, 1960

Anthony Perkins as Norman Bates in *Psycho*

"This time Hitchcock has put his usual close-up face-nibbling sex scene at the very beginning, (as usual, it is quite dispensable) and then goes on to pad the first half of the picture.... The whole thing is, in fact, much too long, and the plot is full of holes.... Two murders and a third attempt are among the most vicious I have ever seen in films, with Hitchcock employing his considerable skill...to shock us past horror-entertainment into resentment." —Stanley Kauffmann, *New Republic,* August 29, 1960

Raging Bull
1980

> DIRECTOR: Martin Scorsese; SCREENPLAY: Paul Schrader, Mardik Martin; CAST: Robert De Niro, Cathy Moriarty, Joe Pesci.
> Selected to the National Film Registry, Library of Congress. Academy Award winner for Best Actor, Editing; nominations for Picture, Director, Supporting Actor, Supporting Actress, Cinematography. Golden Globe winner and New York Film Critics Circle award winner for Best Actor.

"I know I'm supposed to be responding to a powerful, ironic realism, but I just feel trapped. Jake says, 'You dumb f—k,' and Joey says, 'You dumb f—k,' and they repeat it and repeat it.

And I think, What am I doing here watching these two dumb f—ks?" —Pauline Kael, *New Yorker,* December 8, 1980

"...a monomaniacal, crabbed, limited work...The film has distanced us so much from the hero that by the time Sugar Ray wipes him out with a haymaker—an overhand wallop that nearly takes Jake's face off—we're not much moved; it's just gruesome spectacle. *Raging Bull* winds up punishing the audience with its integrity." —David Denby, *New York,* December 1, 1980

"Watching *Raging Bull* is like seeing a skillful documentary on amputation....Whether it is true to the life of Jake La Motta or to boxing is an irrelevant question.

What it says about humanity is skewed, and ultimately a
lie." —Richard A. Blake, *America,* December 20, 1980

Rashomon
1951

> DIRECTOR: Akira Kurosawa; SCREENPLAY: Akira Kurosawa;
> CAST: Toshiro Mifune, Machiko Kyo, Masayuki Mori,
> Takashi Shimura.
> Academy Award winner for Best Foreign Film;
> nomination for Art Direction. Venice Film Festival award for
> Best Film.

"Perhaps I am purblind to the merits of *Rashomon,* but no
matter how enlightened I may become on the art forms
of Nippon, I am going to go on thinking that a Japanese
potpourri of Erskine Caldwell, Stanislavski, and Harpo
Marx isn't likely to provide much sound diversion."
—John McCarten, *New Yorker,* December 29, 1951

Rear Window
1954

> DIRECTOR: Alfred Hitchcock; SCREENPLAY: John Mitchell
> Hayes; CAST: James Stewart, Grace Kelly, Thelma Ritter.
> Academy Award nominations for Best Director,
> Screenplay, Cinematography.

"What isn't understandable...is Alfred Hitchcock's association with this enterprise....I fear that *Rear Window*
must be taken as another example of his footless ambition to make a movie that stands absolutely still....Maybe
one of these days he's going to bust out the way he used
to, and then we'll have some satisfactory films." —John
McCarten, *New Yorker,* August 7, 1954

The Red Shoes
1948

DIRECTOR: Michael Powell, Emeric Pressburger; SCREENPLAY: Michael Powell, Emeric Pressburger; CAST: Anton Walbrook, Moira Shearer, Marius Goring.

Academy Award winner for Best Score; nominations for Best Picture, Original Story, Art Direction, Editing.

"...a lingering, calf-eyed look at backstage ballet's little world of overworked egos and underdone glands...As in most movies that grapple with Art, the burden of the suffering falls on the audience, which is subjected to all the knitted brows, quivering nostrils, tossed locks—and tantrumacious bad manners....*The Red Shoes* is such a spotty piece of movie craftsmanship that it is hard to believe that it is a major effort by Britain's crack moviemaking team, Michael Powell and Emeric Pressburger." —*Time*, October 25, 1948

The Rules of the Game (*La Regle de jeu*)
1939

DIRECTOR: Jean Renoir; SCREENPLAY: Jean Renoir, Carl Koch; CAST: Marcel Dalio, Nora Gregor, Mila Parély, Jean Renoir.

"Exactly what Jean Renoir had in mind when he wrote, performed in, and directed *The Rules of the Game*...is anybody's guess....The new arrival...is really one for the buzzards. Here we have a baffling mixture of stale sophistication, coy symbolism, and galloping slapstick that almost defies analysis....The master has dealt his admirers a pointless, thudding punch below the belt." —Howard Thompson, *New York Times*, April 10, 1950

The Scarlet Empress ————————————————————————
1934

> DIRECTOR: Josef Von Sternberg; SCREENPLAY: Manuel
> Komroff; CAST: Marlene Dietrich, John Lodge, Sam Jaffe.

"The imagination can become a horrible thing indeed
when it is given as much scope and freedom as Von
Sternberg apparently enjoyed while making his version
of the Catherine the Great legend. Or perhaps one had
better say that when, as happens every so often, Hollywood decides to make a mistake, it is able, because of the
vastness of its resources of every kind, to make a truly
colossal mistake." —William Troy, *Nation*, October 3,
1934

"Director Josef von Sternberg has long been famous for
the mannered pretentiousness of his photoplays, but
never has his weakness for ostentation reached the
extremes to be found in *The Scarlet Empress*." —*Literary
Digest*, September 29, 1934

The Searchers ————————————————————————————
1956

> DIRECTOR: John Ford; SCREENPLAY: Frank S. Nugent; CAST:
> John Wayne, Jeffrey Hunter, Natalie Wood, Vera Miles.
>
> Selected to the National Film Registry, Library of
> Congress.

"*The Searchers*, a John Ford desert spectacular in prisma-
tic Vista-Vision, is long on brutality and short on logic or
responsible behavior.... All this could be psychologically
tenable, and even interesting, but Wayne's behavior is
presented as the heroic stuff out of which the West was
made. In fact, the ex-soldier he portrays is a psychotic

with homicidal tendencies which he is given almost unlimited opportunities to indulge, and *The Searchers* is a picture for sadists in very beautiful country." —Robert Hatch, *Nation,* June 23, 1956

The Seventh Seal (*Det Sjunde Inseglet*) ────────
1957

> DIRECTOR: Ingmar Bergman; SCREENPLAY: Ingmar Bergman; CAST: Max von Sydow, Bengt Ekerot, Gunnar Bjornstrand.
> Cannes Film Festival Special Jury Prize winner.

"...an unanswered question is scarcely enough to support a feature length picture, no matter what its style." —Paul V. Beckley, *New York Herald Tribune,* October 14, 1958

"The dialogue, even allowing for possible ineptitude by the English subtitler, is often pretentiously cryptic....Inadequate sets and costumes...Max von Sydow looked too much like a blondined deadpan in the avant garde films made by sex perverts." —Henry Hart, *Films in Review,* November 1958

Shane ─────────────────────────────
1953

> DIRECTOR: George Stevens; SCREENPLAY: A. B Guthrie Jr., from the novel by Jack Schaefer; CAST: Alan Ladd, Jean Arthur, Van Heflin, Jack Palance, Brandon de Wilde.
> Selected to the National Film Registry, Library of Congress. Academy Award winner for Cinematography; nominations for Best Picture, Screenplay, Supporting Actor (Jack Palance, Brandon de Wilde).

"...an incredibly slow Western with a Paul Bunyan type of hero, a pro-homesteaders theme, and the silliest of all child characters." —Manny Farber, *Nation,* July 25, 1953

Snow White and the Seven Dwarfs _____
1937

DIRECTOR: David Hand; SCREENPLAY: Ted Sears, Otto Englander, Earl Hurd, Dorothy Ann Blank, Richard Creedon, Dick Richard, Merrill de Maris, Webb Smith.

Selected to the National Film Registry, Library of Congress. Special Academy Award to Walt Disney for "significant screen innovation."

"At least a third of the film is boring, needlessly and pathetically and uncondonably boring.... That the character Snow White is a failure in every way is undisputable. As a moving figure she is unreal, as a face and body she is absurd, and in terms of what she does she is ludicrous.... Another *Snow White* will sound the Disney death-knell." —V. F. Calverton, *Current History,* June 1938

"As it moved on toward the fifth reel, one began to yawn in mild amusement at this Cecil B. DeMille-ish conception of a fairy tale, and wish Donald Duck would appear from behind somewhere, singing "Hickory Dickory Dock" in that outrageous nasal accent of his." —David Wolff, *New Masses,* January 25, 1938

Some Like It Hot _____
1959

DIRECTOR: Billy Wilder; SCREENPLAY: Billy Wilder, I. A. L. Diamond; CAST: Jack Lemmon, Tony Curtis, Marilyn Monroe, Joe E. Brown.

Selected to the National Film Registry, Library of Congress. Academy Award nominations for Best Screenplay,

Director, Cinematography, Actor, Art Direction; British Academy of Film and Television Arts award for Best Actor (Jack Lemmon). Golden Globe winner for Best Actor (Jack Lemmon), Actress (Marilyn Monroe); Writers Guild of America, West award for Comedy.

"The basic gag of this picture is female impersonation, one of the standbys of old-fashioned burlesque. Tony Curtis and Jack Lemmon are the impersonators, and though they do not make like fairies, Wilder does let the action, and some of the dialogue, run along lines that titillate sex perverts.... For much of *Some Like it Hot* is in very blue taste. There's no excuse—not even the hoary one of entertaining the lowest common denominator." —Ellen Fitzpatrick, *Films in Review*, April 1959

"It does not sound a good idea to mix that gangster mass-murder in Chicago on Saint Valentine's Day in 1929 with a comic idea which draws its inspiration from two men, witnesses of the killing in the garage, disguising themselves as members of a female orchestra; nor is it." —*London Times*, May 14, 1959

La Strada
1954

DIRECTOR: Federico Fellini; SCREENPLAY: Federico Fellini, Ennio Flaiano, Tullio Pinelli; CAST: Giulietta Masina, Anthony Quinn, Richard Basehart.

Academy Award winner for Best Foreign Film; nomination for Best Screenplay.

"Federico Fellini, a comparatively new Italian director, has been much praised in Europe for this not too professional film, largely on the ground that it concerns human loneliness. Since our loneliness is an omnipresent fact we scarcely need to be reminded of it amateurishly.…Fellini's direction left a great deal to be desired. Perhaps he is capable of doing better with a more coherent and significant script." —Diana Willing, *Films in Review,* August/September, 1956

"…there is, alas, a good deal of monotony about his characters. The strong man, played by Anthony Quinn, never, until the long-delayed end, displays anything in the way of human emotion, and the unfortunate girl, played by Giulietta Masina, who has been done up to resemble Harry Langdon, has a limited range of expression, registering joy and sorrow but nothing in between." —John McCarten, *New Yorker,* July 28, 1956

Strangers on a Train
1951

> DIRECTOR: Alfred Hitchcock; SCREENPLAY: Raymond Chandler, Czenzi Ormonde; CAST: Farley Granger, Ruth Roman, Robert Walker, Leo G. Carroll, Patricia Hitchcock.

"Mr. Hitchcock again is tossing a crazy murder story in the air and trying to con us into thinking that it will stand up without support.…His basic premise of fear fired by menace is so thin and so utterly unconvincing that the story just does not stand.…Farley Granger plays the terrified catspaw (as he did in *Rope*) as though he were constantly swallowing his tongue." —Bosley Crowther, *New York Times,* July 4, 1951

Sunset Boulevard
1950

> DIRECTOR: Billy Wilder; SCREENPLAY: Charles Brackett, Billy Wilder, D. M. Marshman Jr.; CAST: Gloria Swanson, William Holden, Erich von Stroheim.

Selected to the National Film Registry, Library of
Congress. Academy Award winner for Best Screenplay,
Score; nominations for Best Picture, Director,
Cinematography, Actress, Actor, Supporting Actor,
Supporting Actress, Editing.

"A pretentious slice of Roquefort...Since *Sunset
Boulevard* contains the germ of a good idea, it's a pity it
was not better written....The Messrs. Charles Brackett,
Billy Wilder, and D. M. Marshman Jr., who fashioned
this tone poem, substituted snappy photography and
dialogue for what could have been a genuinely moving
tragedy....it is peopled with splendid actors...but their
combined highly skilled efforts cannot cover up the
essential hollowness of the enterprise." —Philip
Hamburger, *New Yorker*, August 19, 1950

"The writing throughout is synthetic—wise guy, hol-
lowly disenchanted, pertly humorous, and oddly flat, as
if the smartest cracks of all the hit plays, radio programs,
talking pictures, magazine stories, and cafe anecdotes
were set end to end and passed off as sober statement.
All calculation, the picture reveals no trace of either love
or hate. Its feeling is pure celluloid." —Harold
Clurman, *New Republic*, September 4, 1950

Things to Come
1936

DIRECTOR: William Cameron Menzies; SCREENPLAY: H. G.
Wells, from his book *The Shape of Things to Come*; CAST:
Raymond Massey, Edward Chapman, Ralph Richardson,
Margaretta Scott, Cedric Hardwicke.

"...intolerably prosy and grotesquely unconvincing. I
was confirmed in a former suspicion, namely, that the
future is the dullest subject on earth....The actors

seemed to know this better than Mr. Wells or Mr. Korda did, for they were unable to say their lines as if they meant them; they stared into the abominable blankness around them and said their pieces like children on parents' day." —Mark Van Doren, *Nation,* April 29, 1936

The Third Man
1949

DIRECTOR: Carol Reed; SCREENPLAY: Graham Greene; CAST: Joseph Cotten, Trevor Howard, Alida Valli, Orson Welles.

Academy Award winner for Cinematography; nominations for Director, Editing. British Academy of Film and Television Arts award for Best British Film; Cannes Film Festival Grand Prix winner.

Joseph Cotten and Orson Welles in *The Third Man*

"It bears the usual foreign trademarks...over-elaborated to the point of being a monsterpiece....*The Third Man*'s murky, familiar mood springs chiefly from Graham Greene's script, which proves again that he is an uncinematic snob who has robbed the early Hitchcock of everything but his genius....Greene's story...is like a wheel-less freight train..." —Manny Farber, *Nation*, April 1, 1950

The Treasure of the Sierra Madre
1948

> DIRECTOR: John Huston; SCREENPLAY: John Huston, from the novel by B. Traven; CAST: Humphrey Bogart, Walter Huston, Tim Holt.
>
> Selected to the National Film Registry, Library of Congress. Academy Award winner for Best Director, Screenplay, Supporting Actor; nomination for Best Picture. Golden Globe winner for Director, Picture, Supporting Actor (Walter Huston).

"...even if the premise is granted, the film's methods of elaborating on it are certainly something less than beguiling...the story approaches its inevitable climax—a shot of an empty gold pouch hanging on a cactus—in such a moping manner that it is almost impossible to believe that it was directed by the usually skilled John Huston." —John McCarten, *New Yorker*, January 24, 1948

2001: A Space Odyssey
1968

> DIRECTOR: Stanley Kubrick; SCREENPLAY: Stanley Kubrick, Arthur C. Clarke, from his story *The Sentinel*; CAST: Gary Lockwood, Keir Dullea, William Sylvester, Leonard Rossiter, Douglas Rain.

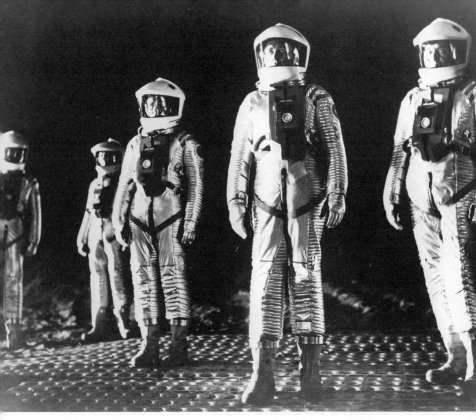

The spacemen examining an excavation on the Moon...*2001*

Selected to the National Film Registry, Library of Congress. Academy Award winner for Special Effects; nominations for Best Screenplay, Director.

"...for all its lively visual and mechanical spectacle, a kind of space-*Spartacus* and, more pretentious still, a shaggy God story." —John Simon, *New Leader*, May 6, 1968

"*2001* is not a cinematic landmark. It compares with, but does not best, previous efforts at filmed science-fiction....It actually belongs to the technically-slick group previously dominated by George Pal and the Japanese." —*Variety*, April 3, 1968

"The movie is so completely absorbed in its own problems, its use of color and space, its fanatical devotion to
science-fiction detail, that it is somewhere between hyp-
notic and immensely boring." —Renata Adler, *New York
Times,* April 4, 1968

Vertigo
1958

DIRECTOR: Alfred Hitchcock; SCREENPLAY: Alec Coppel,
Samuel Taylor; CAST: James Stewart, Kim Novak, Barbara
Bel Geddes.
Selected to the National Film Registry, Library of
Congress.

"The old master, now a slave to television, has turned out
another Hitchcock-and-bull story in which the mystery is
not so much who done it as who cares." —*Time,* June
16, 1958

"Alfred Hitchcock, who produced and directed the
thing, has never before indulged in such farfetched
nonsense." —John McCarten, *New Yorker,* June 7, 1958

"At the risk of sounding slow-witted, I must complain
that Alfred Hitchcock's *Vertigo* was a little too difficult for
me. I had to concentrate so narrowly on the labyrinth of
the plot that I never broke out in the cold sweat which is
the emotional reward of a good thriller." —Robert
Hatch, *Nation,* June 14, 1958

"...it pursues its theme of false identity with such plodding persistence that, by the time the climactic cat is let
out of the bag, the audience has long since had kit-
tens..." —Arthur Knight, *Saturday Review,* June 7, 1958

The Wizard of Oz ────────────────────
1939

DIRECTOR: Victor Fleming; SCREENPLAY: Noel Langley,
Florence Ryerson, Edgar Allan Wolfe, from the book by
Frank L. Baum; CAST: Judy Garland, Frank Morgan, Ray
Bolger, Jack Haley, Bert Lahr, Margaret Hamilton, Billie
Burke, Charley Grapewin, Clara Blandick.

**Ray Bolger, Jack Haley, Judy Garland, and Bert Lahr
in** *The Wizard of Oz*

Selected to the National Film Registry, Library of Congress. Academy Award nomination for Best Picture.

"It has dwarfs, music, Technicolor, freak characters, and Judy Garland. It can't be expected to have a sense of humor as well—and as for the light touch of fantasy, it weighs like a pound of fruitcake soaking wet." —Otis Ferguson, *New Republic*, September 20, 1939

"Displays no trace of imagination, good taste, or ingenuity... I say it's a stinkeroo. The vulgarity of which I was conscious all through the film is difficult to analyze. Part of it was the raw, eye-straining Technicolor, applied with a complete lack of restraint." —Russell Maloney, *New Yorker*, August 19, 1939

Wuthering Heights
1939

DIRECTOR: William Wyler; SCREENPLAY: Ben Hecht, Charles MacArthur, from the novel by Emily Brontë; CAST: Merle Oberon, Laurence Olivier, David Niven, Flora Robson, Donald Crisp, Geraldine Fitzgerald.

Academy Award winner for Cinematography; nominations for Best Picture, Actor, Screenplay, Score, Director, Supporting Actress (Geraldine Fitzgerald), Art Direction.

"Its general sombreness and psychological tragedy is too heavy for general appeal.... It's rather dull material for general audiences." —*Variety*, March 29, 1939

"How much better they would have made *Wuthering Heights* in France. They know there how to shoot sexual passion, but in this Californian-constructed Yorkshire,

among the sensitive neurotic English voices, sex is cel-
lophaned; there is no egotism, no obsession.... So a lot of
reverence has gone into a picture which should have
been as coarse as a sewer." —Graham Greene, *Spectator,*
May 5, 1939

2

Who Listens to the Critics Anyway?

Scathing Reviews of the Most Popular Movies of All Time

Alien
1979

> DIRECTOR: Ridley Scott; SCREENPLAY: Dan O'Bannon; CAST: Tom Skerritt, Sigourney Weaver, John Hurt, Veronica Cartwright, Harry Dean Stanton, Ian Holm, Yaphet Kotto.
> One of the top five box-office hits of 1979.

"This sci-fi horror epic is an overblown B-movie.... Technically impressive but awfully portentous and as difficult to sit through as a Black Mass sung in Latin.... *Alien,* like *Dawn of the Dead,* only scares you away from the movies." —Michael Sragow, *Los Angeles Herald Examiner,* May 25, 1979

All the President's Men
1976

> DIRECTOR: Alan J. Pakula; SCREENPLAY: William Goldman, from the book by Carl Bernstein and Bob Woodward; CAST:

Robert Redford, Dustin Hoffman, Jason Robards Jr., Martin
Balsam, Hal Holbrook, Jane Alexander.

One of the top five box-office hits of 1976. Academy
Award winner for Best Screenplay, Supporting Actor (Jason
Robards Jr.); nominations for Best Picture, Director,
Supporting Actress (Jane Alexander).

"Pakula's howitzer-sized sound effects don't really convince us that what we are seeing tells us much about
Watergate. But then, his plot doesn't convince us that
what we are seeing tells us much about Woodward and
Bernstein, either. I don't know—the whole thing smells
like a cover-up to me." —Colin Westerbeck Jr.,
Commonweal, April 23, 1976

American Graffiti
1973

DIRECTOR: George Lucas; SCREENPLAY: George Lucas; CAST:
Richard Dreyfuss, Ronny Howard, Paul Le Mat, Charlie
Martin Smith, Cindy Williams, Candy Clark, Mackenzie
Philips.

One of the top five box-office hits of 1973. Academy
Award nominations for Best Picture, Screenplay, Director,
Supporting Actress (Candy Clark).

"For whom was it 'just like that,' I wonder...Only for
white middle-class boys whose memories have turned
into pop...mechanical people, including searching
young men, are a blight on the movies—evidence that
the filmmakers aren't thinking freshly, that they're re-
sorting to the stockpile." —Pauline Kael, *New Yorker*,
October 29, 1973

Back to the Future ──────────────
1985

> DIRECTOR: Robert Zemeckis; SCREENPLAY: Robert Zemeckis,
> Bob Gale; CAST: Michael J. Fox, Christopher Lloyd, Crispin
> Glover.
>   Top box-office hit of 1985. Academy Award nomination
> for Original Screenplay.

"...yet another in a series of endless close encounters of
the Steven Spielberg kind. Someday movies may return
to normal. Meanwhile we're stuck with bubble-gum
fantasies conceived by people who have OD'd on comic
books....The smell of an equally silly sequel permeates
the air like a gas leak." —Rex Reed, *New York Post*,
July 3, 1985

Bambi ──────────────────────
1942

> DIRECTOR: David Hand
>   Top box-office hit of 1942.

"The new Disney cartoon *Bambi* is interesting because it's
the first one that's been entirely unpleasant....Mickey
wouldn't be caught dead in this." —Manny Farber, *New
Republic*, June 29, 1942

Batman ──────────────────────
1989

> DIRECTOR: Tim Burton; SCREENPLAY: Sam Hamm, Warren
> Skaaren; CAST: Michael Keaton, Jack Nicholson, Kim
> Basinger, Billy Dee Williams, Pat Hingle, Jack Palance.

One of the top ten box-office hits of all time.

"*Batman* just sits up there drinking money and serving as a platform for Jack Nicholson's campaign to win an Academy Award nomination. Nicholson is huge; why wasn't the movie called *Joker?* When it's over you're thinking, Bat*who?*" —Stephen Hunter, *Baltimore Evening Sun,* June 23, 1989

Ben-Hur
1959

> DIRECTOR: William Wyler; SCREENPLAY: Karl Tunberg; CAST: Charlton Heston, Haya Harareet, Jack Hawkins, Stephen Boyd, Hugh Griffith, Sam Jaffe.
>
> Top box-office hit of 1959. Winner of 11 Academy Awards, including Best Picture, Director, Actor, Supporting Actor, Cinematography, Art Direction, Editing; winner of the British Academy of Film and Television Arts award for Best Film; Golden Globe winner for Best Picture (Drama) and Best Director; Directors Guild of America award for Best Director.

"I found *Ben-Hur* bloody in every way—bloody bloody and bloody boring. Watching it was like waiting at a railroad crossing while an interminable freight train lumbers past....There was not even a decent, or indecent, Roman orgy, the only valid excuse for making a Biblical picture. Instead of sex, *Ben-Hur* gives us sadism....In short, here is a film that tries to debauch whatever taste, feeling or simple common sense Hollywood and television have left us." —Dwight Macdonald, *Esquire,* March 1960

Beverly Hills Cop ————————————————
1984

> DIRECTOR: Martin Brest; SCREENPLAY: Daniel Petrie Jr.; CAST:
> Eddie Murphy, Judge Reinhold, Lisa Eilbacher, Bronson
> Pinchot.
> One of the top ten box-office hits of all time. Academy
> Award nomination for Best Original Screenplay.

"...with Murphy busting his sides gaffawing in self-congratulation, and the camera jammed into his tonsils, damned if the audience doesn't whoop and carry on as if yes, this is a wow of a comedy...Murphy's aggressive oneupmanship through most of the film kills your interest in him as a performer" —Pauline Kael, *New Yorker*, December 24, 1984

Blazing Saddles ————————————————
1974

> DIRECTOR: Mel Brooks; SCREENPLAY: Norman Steinberg, Mel
> Brooks, Andrew Bergman, Richard Pryor, Alan Unger;
> CAST: Cleavon Little, Gene Wilder, Madeline Kahn, Harvey
> Corman, Slim Pickens.
> One of the top five box-office hits of 1974. Academy
> Award nominations for Best Supporting Actress (Madeline
> Kahn), Song.

"I never imagined I'd think back longingly on Brooks's first film, *The Producers*—but it never sank to this....as a director he doesn't have enough style to make the unfunny funny. In *Blazing Saddles* he makes the unfunny desperate." —Pauline Kael, *New Yorker*, February 18, 1974

"No mention of *Blazing Saddles* can be brief enough.... It is like playing tennis not only without a net but also without a court, and with two balls simultaneously." — John Simon, *Esquire,* May 1974

Butch Cassidy and the Sundance Kid _____
1969

> DIRECTOR: George Roy Hill; SCREENPLAY: William Goldman; CAST: Paul Newman, Robert Redford, Katharine Ross, Strother Martin.
>
> Top box-office hit of 1969. Academy Award winner for Best Screenplay, Cinematography, Score, Song; nominations for Best Picture, Director.

"Every character, every scene, is marred by the film's double view, which oscillates between sympathy and farce.... Director George Roy Hill abruptly annihilates the nostalgia with a scat-singing sound track by Burt Bacharach at his most cacophonous. Coupled with a mod love song, "Raindrops Keep Falling on My Head"...the score makes the film as absurd and anachronistic as the celebrated Smothers Brothers cowboy who played the kerosene-powered guitar." —*Time,* September 26, 1969

The Caine Mutiny _____
1954

> DIRECTOR: Edward Dmytryk; SCREENPLAY: Stanley Roberts, from the novel by Herman Wouk; CAST: Humphrey Bogart, Jose Ferrer, Van Johnson, Fred MacMurray.
>
> One of the top five box-office hits of 1954. Academy Award nominations for Best Picture, Screenplay, Score,

Actor (Humphrey Bogart), Supporting Actor (Tom Tully), Editing.

"Bogart is not convincing....Dmytryk's direction is defective.... The court martial itself, which is exploited so dramatically on the stage, is thrown away in the film....If Hollywood films are to continue to gnaw at the intangibles which support our armed forces...let them, at least, be as well-made and as cinematic as *From Here to Eternity.*" —Henrietta Lehman, *Films in Review,* June/July 1954

Cheaper By the Dozen
1950

DIRECTOR: Walter Lang; SCREENPLAY: Lamar Trotti, from the book by Frank B. Gilbreth Jr. and Ernestine Gilbreth Carey; CAST: Clifton Webb, Myrna Loy, Jeanne Crain, Edgar Buchanan.

One of the top five box-office hits of 1950.

"...as Mr. Webb is an eccentric joke and Miss Loy evidently fed to the back teeth with the whole thing, and as their offspring are too numerous to be anything but amorphous, they, to put it mildly, fail in their endeavour. Directed by Mr. Walter Lang in Technicolor, this comedy is a desert of wasted talent, and one is far more inclined to weep than laugh...." —Virgina Graham, *Spectator,* May 5, 1950

"A plotless string of mild, rambling anecdotes, with Clifton ('Belvedere') Webb miscast in the central role, it is not much more fun than leafing through somebody else's family album." —*Time,* April 10, 1950

Close Encounters of the Third Kind _____
1977

> DIRECTOR: Steven Spielberg; SCREENPLAY: Steven Spielberg;
> CAST: Richard Dreyfuss, François Truffaut, Teri Garr,
> Melinda Dillon.
> One of the top five box-office hits of 1977. Academy
> Award winner for Cinematography; nominations for Best
> Director, Score, Supporting Actress.

"Spielberg—which in German means toy mountain—
may indeed have made the most monumental molehill in
movie history, conveniently cone-shaped to serve as a
dunce's cap for an extremely swelled head." —John
Simon, from his collection *Reverse Angle*, 1982

"...the movie is no good. Certainly it has moments that
suggest the tremendous talent, effort and expense that
went into the making but they, alas, only point up the
difference between what is and what might have
been.... To call the project 'ambitious' is to resort to
ironic understatement. 'Impossible' comes closer to the
truth." —Susan Stark, *Detroit Free Press*, November 14,
1977

Deliverance _____
1972

> DIRECTOR: John Boorman; SCREENPLAY: James Dickey, from
> his novel; CAST: Jon Voight, Burt Reynolds, Ned Beatty,
> Ronny Cox, Billy McKinney, Herbert Coward.
> One of the top five box-office hits of 1972. Academy
> Award nominations for Best Picture, Director, Film Editing.

"No performance deserves comment.... There is funda-
mentally no view of the material, just a lot of painful
grasping and groping. The glory-of-nature shots are

trite, the drama is clumsy, and the editing clanks. It's difficult for a film that is not very tightly knit to unravel, but this one does." —Stanley Kauffmann, *New Republic,* August 5, 1972

"*Deliverance* can be considered a stark, uncompromising showdown between basic survival instincts against the character pretensions of a mannered and material society. Unfortunately for John Boorman's heavy film...it can just as easily be argued as a virile, mountain country transposition of nihilistic, specious philosophizing which exploits rather than explores its moments of violent drama." —*Variety,* July 19, 1972

Die Hard
1965

> DIRECTOR: John McTiernan; SCREENPLAY: Jeb Stuart, Steven E. DeSouza; CAST: Bruce Willis, Bonnie Bedelia, Reginald VelJohnson, Paul Gleason, De'Voreaux White, Alan Rickman, Alexander Godunov.

"First there was Sylvester Stallone, then came Arnold Schwarzennegger, and now—Bruce Willis. *Bruce Willis?* Not exactly a name that springs immediately to mind when thinking of muscles 'n' mayhem movies. But such distinctions mean little to the perpetrators of *Die Hard,* the noisiest, ugliest, and most relentlessly stupid movie of the year." —David Ehrenstein, *Los Angeles Herald Examiner,* July 15, 1988

Dr. Zhivago
1965

> DIRECTOR: David Lean; SCREENPLAY: Robert Bolt, from the novel by Boris Pasternak; CAST: Omar Sharif, Julie Christie, Rod Steiger, Alec Guinness, Rita Tushingham, Ralph

Richardson, Tom Courtenay, Geraldine Chaplin, Siobhan McKenna.

One of the top five box-office hits of 1965. Academy Award winner for Best Cinematography, Screenplay, Original Score; nominations for Best Picture, Director, Supporting Actor. Winner of Golden Globe awards for Best Director, Picture, Score, Screenplay.

"It isn't shoddy (except for the music), it isn't soap opera; it's stately, respectable, and dead....It's like watching a gigantic task of stone masonry, executed by unmoved movers. It's not art, it's heavy labor—which, of course, many people respect more than art." —Pauline Kael, from her collection *Kiss Kiss Bang Bang,* 1968

"...the biggest disappointment of 1965...There is nothing holding the effects together, not an idea, or a feeling, or a mood, or even much of a plot, and a relatively capable cast struggles helplessly with Robert Bolt's disconnected, uninspired dialogue as the film bumbles along to boredom." —Andrew Sarris, *Village Voice,* December 30, 1965

"David Lean is a good academic director who collects Oscars as others collect stamps and has given the film epic a more sober, intelligent reputation than it used to have. His film of *Dr. Zhivago* is sober all right, but it isn't very much more, one of those sadly middling films that have obviously been pored and prayed over, but haven't quite got where they meant to...a pedestrian piece..." —Isabel Quigley, *Spectator,* April 29, 1966

"Mr. Bolt has reduced the vast upheaval of the Russian Revolution to the banalities of a doomed romance....the necessities of drama—of action and suspense—are not served by the fact that these two people and some others are possessed by a strange passivity.... This may be faithful to Pasternak, but it makes for painfully slow going and inevitable tedium in a film." —Bosley Crowther, *New York Times,* December 23, 1965

E.T. the Extra-Terrestrial
1982

> DIRECTOR: Steven Spielberg; SCREENPLAY: Melissa Mathison; CAST: Dee Wallace, Henry Thomas, Peter Coyote, Robert MacNaughton, Drew Barrymore.
>
> Top box-office hit of all time. Academy Award winner for Visual Effects, Score, Sound; nominations for Best Picture, Director, Screenplay, Cinematography, Editing.

"*E.T.* is really *Lassie* in science fiction drag.... I was so flabbergasted by Spielberg and Mathison's transparent manipulativeness that I didn't have time to react with the mindless emotionalism that has clouded the acuity of supposedly sharp-eyed critics like Pauline Kael, who found the film 'enchanting.' 'Sappy' or 'simple-minded' would be more accurate." —Robert Asahina, *New Leader,* July 1982

"There is fun Disney would have been proud of in this brilliantly manipulative movie. But to weep at a celebration of infantilism, however fancied up with intimation of innocence? A good laugh's one thing; and so is a good cry. *E.T.* is a far, far cry, a bleat rather, self-pitying, for the moon. Or a moon-toy." —John Coleman, *New Statesman,* December 10, 1982

"The movie moves so fast, the images are so dramatic, and the sound track is so loud that we miss the sexist fireworks on display.... Movies like this are not a balm in

E.T.

our impossible times; they simply make matters worse by repeating the crimes that got us here in the first place. We should all stop believing in fairies until someone makes a film in which little girls have adventures on bicycles, too." —Phyllis Deutsch, *Jump Cut,* April 1983

The Egg and I
1947

> DIRECTOR: Chester Erskine; SCREENPLAY: Chester Erskine,
> Fred Finklehoffe, from the book by Betty Macdonald; CAST:
> Claudette Colbert, Fred MacMurray, Marjorie Main, Percy
> Kilbride.
> One of the top five box-office hits of 1947. Academy
> Award nomination for Best Supporting Actress (Marjorie
> Main).

"An example of just how inaccurate, how unfeeling, how
unreal and how unfunny a movie can be...When you get
out of *The Egg and I* you won't want even to smell fresh
air." —Shirley O'Hara, *New Republic*, May 12, 1947

"Marjorie Main, in an occasional fit of fine, wild comedy,
picks the show up and brandishes it as if she were
wringing its neck. I wish to God she had."
—James Agee, *Nation*, May 10, 1947

The Empire Strikes Back
1980

> DIRECTOR: Irving Kershner; SCREENPLAY: Leigh Brackett,
> Lawrence Kasdan; CAST: Mark Hamill, Harrison Ford,
> Carrie Fisher.
> Top box-office hit of 1980. Winner of Special Achievement
> Academy Award for Special Effects; nominations for Best
> Score, Art Direction.

"*The Empire Strikes Back*...is malodorous offal....
everything is stale, limp, desperately stretched out, and
pretentious....Harrison Ford (Han) offers loutishness
for charm and becomes the epitome of the interstellar
drugstore cowboy. Mark Hamill (Luke) is still the talent-

less Tom Sawyer of outer space—wide-eyed, narrow-minded, strait-laced. Worst of all is Carrie Fisher, whose Leia is a cosmic Shirley Temple but without the slightest acting ability or vestige of prettiness. Though still very young, she looks, without recourse to special effects, as least fifty—the film's only true, albeit depressing, miracle." —John Simon, *National Review,* June 13, 1980

Father of the Bride
1950

> DIRECTOR: Vincente Minnelli; SCREENPLAY: Frances
> Goodrich, Albert Hackett; CAST: Spencer Tracy, Joan
> Bennett, Elizabeth Taylor.
>   One of the top five box-office hits of 1950. Academy
> Award nominations for Best Picture, Screenplay, Actor.

"Since the plot consists simply of outlining the difficulties of putting on a wedding, including, of course, the damnable expense of it all, it grows a little tiresome after a half hour or so.... This may fetch some susceptible ladies in the crowd, but I think it will be hard on everybody else." —John McCarten, *New Yorker,* May 27, 1950

Fiddler on the Roof
1971

> DIRECTOR: Norman Jewison; SCREENPLAY: Joseph Stein;
> CAST: Topol, Norma Crane, Leonard Frey, Molly Picon.
>   Top box-office hit of 1971. Academy Award winner for
> Cinematography, Score; nominations for Best Picture,
> Director, Actor (Topol), Supporting Actor (Leonard Frey).

"It is with a sizable thud that *Fiddler on the Roof* reaches the screen, a great Goliath of a musical toppled by its own size and weight.... Topol, who has a powerful if unpleasantly harsh voice and a commanding presence, is trapped in this big production like a tomato in aspic.... His sense of comedy, matched with Jewison's own cement touch, crushes the fun out of every good line.... The rest of the cast is equally unappealing." —Paul D. Zimmerman, *Newsweek,* November 15, 1971

"Gone with barely a trace are warmth, joy, insight, and even the most elementary kind of entertainment.... Most sorely missed is the magisterial Zero Mostel in the role of Tevye.... He has been replaced for unfathomable reasons by the Israeli star Topol, who labors under the handicap of having to project great amounts of charm and personality when he has none to spare. The credits for *Fiddler* list Norman Jewison as producer and director. On the basis of this and past efforts... he might better be called an anaesthetist."   —Jay Cocks, *Time,* November 22, 1971

From Here to Eternity
1953

> DIRECTOR: Fred Zinnemann; SCREENPLAY: Daniel Taradash, from the novel by James Jones; CAST: Burt Lancaster, Deborah Kerr, Frank Sinatra, Donna Reed, Ernest Borgnine, Montgomery Clift.
>
> One of the top five box-office hits of 1953. Academy Award for Best Picture, Screenplay, Director, Cinematography, Supporting Actor (Frank Sinatra), Supporting Actress; nominations for Actor, Actress, Supporting Actor (Montgomery Clift), Score.

"...granting for the moment the validity of the original materials, I found the movie so riddled with script inconsistencies and weird casting that it was impossible to take it seriously.... Altogether, while I am more than normally receptive to pictures that eschew false glamor and artificially imposed happy endings, this one seemed merely sordid." —Moira Walsh, *America*, August 15, 1953

The Fugitive
1993

DIRECTOR: Andrew Davis; SCREENPLAY: David N. Twohy, Jeb Stuart; CAST: Harrison Ford, Tommy Lee Jones.

One of the top five box-office hits of 1993. Academy Award winner for Best Supporting Actor (Tommy Lee Jones); nomination for Best Picture, Screenplay, Cinematography, Editing. Golden Globe winner for Best Actor, Supporting Actor, Director. Winner of the Directors Guild of America award for Best Director.

"Perhaps the best cure for a cinematic beau geste as strenuously unsatisfying as *The Fugitive* is to take two aspirins and pray for amnesia the next morning...." —*Washington Times*, August 6, 1993

Funny Girl
1968

DIRECTOR: William Wyler; SCREENPLAY: Isobel Lennart, from her play; CAST: Barbra Streisand, Omar Sharif, Walter Pidgeon, Kay Medford.

Top box-office hit of 1968. Academy Award winner for Best Actress; nominations for Best Picture, Cinematography, Musical Direction, Supporting Actress, Song.

"*Funny Girl* is the ultimate expression of Barbra in all her barbaric solitude. The rest of the movie is a desert of destroyed egos. Omar Sharif's Nick Arnstein comes over as a two-legged cocker spaniel with a ruffled shirtfront..." —Andrew Sarris, *Village Voice*, October 10, 1968

Ghost
1990

DIRECTOR: Jerry Zucker; SCREENPLAY: Bruce Joel Rubin; CAST: Patrick Swayze, Demi Moore, Tony Goldwyn, Whoopi Goldberg.

Top box-office hit of 1990. Academy Award winner for Best Supporting Actress, Screenplay; nominations for Best Picture, Score, Editing.

"The film would have you believe that it is about love surviving beyond the grave, but these two could never be mistaken for Heathcliff and Cathy. All their charms cannot change the fact that they are unsympathetic yuppie types living in Soho.... If we strip away the ghost story, and look at the underlying raison d'etre of *Ghost*, the story of revenge, we still come up empty."
—Maria Garcia, *Films in Review*, October 1990

Giant
1956

DIRECTOR: George Stevens; SCREENPLAY: Fred Guiol, Ivan Moffat, from the novel by Edna Ferber; CAST: Rock Hudson, Elizabeth Taylor, James Dean, Mercedes McCambridge.

One of the top five box-office hits of 1956. Academy Award winner for Best Director; nominations for Best Picture, Screenplay, Score, Actor, Supporting Actress, Art Direction, Editing.

"*Giant* is a mistake George Stevens must be forgiven for.... I think he probably suffered acutely while he was making it. His despair seemed to me to be most apparent

when he was most shoddy, when, e.g., he would let
Tiomkin's sound track blare crash down on a cut to
nothing more dramatic than a cat. My admiration for
Stevens prevents me from enumerating the other
shoddy tricks by which this great director tried to give an
amorphous mass of piffle occasional vitality."
—Courtland Phipps, *Films in Review,* November 1956

Goldfinger
1964

> DIRECTOR: Guy Hamilton; SCREENPLAY: Richard Maibaum,
> Paul Dehn from the novel by Ian Fleming; CAST: Sean
> Connery, Honor Blackman, Gert Frobe, Harold Sakata,
> Shirley Eaton, Bernard Lee.
>
> One of the top five box-office hits of 1964.

Old Double-Oh Seven is slipping—or, rather, his script
writers are....This is tediously apparent in
Goldfinger....in this most gaudy of his outings...he manages to bestow his male attentions on only a couple of
passing supplicants...Neither is up to the standard of
femininity usually maintained for Mr. Bond....what
they give us in *Goldfinger* is an excess of science-fiction
fun, a mess of mechanical melodrama, and a minimum
of bedroom farce."   —Bosley Crowther, *New York Times,*
December 22, 1964

The Graduate
1967

> DIRECTOR: Mike Nichols; SCREENPLAY: Calder Willingham,
> Buck Henry; CAST: Dustin Hoffman, Anne Bancroft,
> Katharine Ross.
>
> Top box-office hit of 1967. Academy Award winner for
> Best Director; nominations for Best Picture, Screenplay,
> Cinematography, Actor, Actress, Supporting Actress.

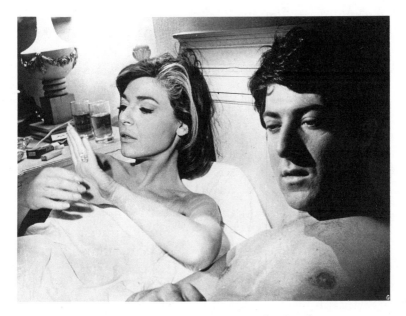

Anne Bancroft and Dustin Hoffman in *The Graduate*

"The movie as a whole is a Youth-grooving movie for old people....Maybe Nichols does have the talent to do something more important—so far he has the energy and the ambition—but we're not going to find out as long as an evasive gimmicky hoax like *The Graduate* is trumpeted as a milestone in American film history." —Stephen Farber and Estelle Changas, *Film Quarterly,* Spring 1968

Grease
1978

> DIRECTOR: Randal Kleiser; SCREENPLAY: Bronte Woodard, from the stage musical by Jim Jacobs, Warren Casey; CAST: John Travolta, Olivia Newton-John, Stockard Channing, Eve Arden, Sid Caesar.
>
> Top box-office hit of 1978.

"Paramount invited me to a preview at one of New York's biggest neighborhood popcorn houses, so I thought, what the hell. And a kind of hell it turned out to be....the sound track blasts away at a decibel level you might expect to encounter if trapped in an elevator with a transistor-equipped messenger boy....Though *Grease* is obviously intended to effervesce with adolescent joy of life, its unifying human characteristic is stupidity expressed in hysteria—a not very merry conceit."
—Robert Hatch, *Nation*, July 1, 1978

"It has no book to speak of. To put it another way, the book is unspeakable. The music goes in one ear and out the same ear. It has no kind of focus in atmosphere or tone, it doesn't even have a *look*. It's just a sort of floating insult, shopping for a subject to light on." —Stanley Kauffmann, *New Republic*, July 1, 1978

Gremlins
1984

> DIRECTOR: Joe Dante; SCREENPLAY: Chris Columbus; CAST: Zach Galligan, Phoebe Cates, Hoyt Axton, Polly Holliday, Keye Luke.
> One of the top five box-office hits of 1984.

Gremlins is a nightmare.... It is aimed at children, but its gory conflicts will scare them out of their wits.... For example, how is an audience to react to the girl who explains that she hates Christmas because her father got stuck in the chimney while playing Santa Claus and his decomposing body was discovered several days later? Ho-ho-ho. Wake me up, please." —Richard A. Blake, *America*, June 30, 1984

"If it was to be expected that *Gremlins* would gross more than $100 million within six weeks of opening...what does come as a surprise is the movie's unmitigated awfulness....As far as I can see, this movie won't do any good and it might even do some harm: It could put a dent in any eight-or-ten-year-old's moral development." —Daphne Merkin, *New Leader,* July 9 & 23, 1984

Home Alone
1990

>   DIRECTOR: Chris Columbus; SCREENPLAY: John Hughes;
>   CAST: Macauley Culkin, Joe Pesci, Daniel Stern, Catherine
>   O'Hara, John Heard, John Candy.
>   One of the top ten box-office hits of all time.

"So it's unbelievable, but is it amusing? The answer is no, unless you're a fan of mean-spirited, sub-Stooges slapstick....Culkin...is reasonably appealing, though there's no way he or any other actor could make this character or situation credible....Better to stay home alone than to go out and see *Home Alone.*" —Tom Jacobs, *Los Angeles Daily News,* November 16, 1990

The Hunchback of Notre Dame
1939

>   DIRECTOR: William Dieterle; SCREENPLAY: Sonya Levien,
>   Bruno Frank, from the novel by Victor Hugo; CAST: Charles
>   Laughton, Sir Cedric Hardwicke, Thomas Mitchell, Maureen
>   O'Hara, Edmond O'Brien, Alan Marshal.
>   One of the top five box-office hits of 1939.

The Hunchback of Notre Dame, all expense and care and dramatic possibilities considered, is my candidate for the worst-made Class-A film of a year.... The excitement was exciting when they got to it at last—but the audience was already too limp and damp to rise to anything, except to go home." —Otis Ferguson, *New Republic*, January 22, 1940

Indiana Jones and the Temple of Doom _____
1984

> DIRECTOR: Steven Spielberg; SCREENPLAY: Willard Huyck, Gloria Katz; CAST: Harrison Ford, Kate Capshaw, Ke Huy Kwan.
>
> One of the top five box-office hits of 1984.

"Moviegoers deserve more than the racism, sexism, and all-purpose mayhem on view here.... The message is plain: White people are good, yellow people are shifty, brown people are weak or sinister. Some lesson for the '80s!" —David Sterritt, *Christian Science Monitor*, May 31, 1984

"...a cinematic variant on the theme of the 'white man's burden'... It powerfully reinforces the depiction of the white man as the paternalistic defender of justice against oppression and of the civilized order against primordial female chaos...." —Moishe Postone and Elizabeth Traube, *Jump Cut*, March 1985

"...inordinately racist and sexist, even by Hollywood standards. There's a kind of willful ignorance here, as though the magnitude of their success exempts Lucas and Spielberg from any moral considerations. Like white boys just want to have fun!" —J. Hoberman, *Village Voice*, June 5, 1984

Jaws
1975

DIRECTOR: Steven Spielberg; SCREENPLAY: Carl Gottlieb, Peter Benchley, from his novel; CAST: Roy Scheider, Robert Shaw, Richard Dreyfuss, Lorraine Gary, Murray Hamilton.

Top box-office hit of 1975. Academy Award winner for Best Score, Film Editing; nomination for Best Picture. Winner of the British Academy of Film and Television Arts and Golden Globe awards for Best Score.

"The ads show a gaping shark's mouth. If sharks can yawn, that's presumably what this one is doing. It's certainly what I was doing all through this picture, even in those few moments when I was frightened."
—Stanley Kauffmann, *New Republic,* July 26, 1975

Lethal Weapon
1987

DIRECTOR: Richard Donner; SCREENPLAY: Shane Black; CAST: Mel Gibson, Danny Glover, Gary Busey, Mitchell Ryan, Tom Atkins.

"As a thriller, it lacks logic. As a cop film, it throws standard police procedures, and with them any hope of authenticity, to the wind. As a showcase for the martial arts, it's a disappointment....And as action-adventure, it's pointlessly puerile." —Johanna Steinmetz, *Chicago Tribune,* March 6, 1987

M*A*S*H
1970

DIRECTOR: Robert Altman; SCREENPLAY: Ring Lardner Jr., from the novel by Richard Hooker; CAST: Donald Sutherland, Elliott Gould, Tom Skerritt, Sally Kellerman, Robert Duvall.

One of the top five box-office hits of 1970. Academy
Award for Best Screenplay; nominations for Best Picture,
Director, Supporting Actress.

"At the end, the film simply runs out of steam, says good-
by to its major characters, and calls final attention to
itself as a movie—surely the saddest and most overworked of cop-out devices in the comic film reper-
tory." —Roger Greenspun, *New York Times,* January 26,
1970

The Music Man
1962

> DIRECTOR: Morton da Costa; SCREENPLAY: Marion Hargrove,
> from the book by Meredith Willson; CAST: Robert Preston,
> Shirley Jones, Buddy Hackett.
>
> One of the top five box-office hits of 1962. Academy
> Award nomination for Best Picture.

"...overacted, overcute, overloud, and overlong...*Music
Man* operates on the principle that an audience that is hit
hard enough, often enough, can be reduced to a pulp of
pleasure." —*Time,* July 20, 1962

National Lampoon's Animal House
1978

> DIRECTOR: John Landis; SCREENPLAY: Harold Ramis, Douglas
> Kenney, Chris Miller; CAST: John Belushi, Tim Matheson,
> John Vernon.
>
> One of the top five box-office hits of 1978.

America is vast, and so, my goodness, are the insults
launched against its educational system....*Animal House*

depicts a university life that is deeply anti-academic, an undergraduate life that is as blind as a pit pony, and an almost criminally false idea of the national sense of the comedic." —Penelope Gilliatt, *New Yorker,* August 14, 1978

Nine to Five
1980

DIRECTOR: Colin Higgins; SCREENPLAY: Colin Higgins, Patricia Resnick; CAST: Jane Fonda, Dolly Parton, Lily Tomlin, Dabney Coleman.

One of the top five box-office hits of 1980.

"*Nine to Five* is a vile mess, but it may find its audience— the one that has made *Airplane!* and *Private Benjamin* two of the year's top-grossing films. Some people will go anywhere for a laugh, and Higgins will go to any lengths to get them." —Richard Corliss, *Time,* December 22, 1980

"Feminists should be appalled by this odious and obnoxious comedy." —Robert Asahina, *New Leader,* December 29, 1980

"One can sense that behind the ugly clowning, the female-caper-movie episodes, someone is trying to say something serious about politics and feminism, but the movie is a witless mess, a nastier *I Love Lucy.* The filmmakers treat us like stupid children, yet I know some people will hail this nonsensical picture as an advance for women. In this country, righteous opportunism goes a long way." —David Denby, *New York,* December 22, 1980

The Odd Couple
1968

> DIRECTOR: Gene Saks; SCREENPLAY: Neil Simon, from his play; CAST: Jack Lemmon, Walter Matthau.
>
> One of the top five box-office hits of 1968. Academy Award nomination for Best Screenplay.

Jack Lemmon is one of our best comedians, a gifted actor, and a fine human being, but he should stop accepting the kind of scripts he does. In this one he merely stooges for Walter Matthau, an actor of incomparably smaller range. And the script!... The characterizations are uninteresting; the dialogue is middle-middle class Riverside Drive...."   —Harriet Gibbs, *Films in Review,* June/July 1968

"...if the play was like the movie, I can't see what all the shouting was about... For a while the episode with the girls upstairs relieves the tedium, but even that wears thin. *The Odd Couple* may be interesting as an idea; as a movie with movement, it's only a static idea."   —Philip T. Hartung, *Commonweal,* May 17, 1968

The Omen
1976

> DIRECTOR: Richard Donner; SCREENPLAY: David Seltzer; CAST: Gregory Peck, Lee Remick, David Warner, Billie Whitelaw, Leo McKern.

"There seems to exist a special kennel in Hollywood where pictures that were artistic dogs but popular successes are crossbred for the delectation of the great unwashed, and the even keener delight of the money men. Possibly the highest stud fees of the moment go to that champion hellhound, *The Exorcist*, and the prize bitch *Rosemary's Baby*, whose latest whelp, *The Omen*, is certainly all dog from snout to tail..." —John Simon, *New York*, July 12, 1976

The Paleface
1948

> DIRECTOR: Norman Z. McLeod; SCREENPLAY: Edmund Hartman, Frank Tashlin; CAST: Bob Hope, Jane Russell, Robert Armstrong.
> One of the top five box-office hits of 1948.

"Just a second-string 'Road' show, at best, conspicuously lacking the presence of Bing Crosby and Dorothy Lamour..." —Bosley Crowther, *New York Times*, December 16, 1948

Peyton Place
1957

> DIRECTOR: Mark Robson; SCREENPLAY: John Michael Hayes, from the novel by Grace Metalious; CAST: Lana Turner, Arthur Kennedy, Hope Lange, Lee Philips, Lloyd Nolan, Russ Tamblyn, Diane Varsi.
> One of the top five box-office hits of 1957. Academy Award nominations for Best Picture, Screenplay, Director, Cinematography, Actor, Actress, Supporting Actor, Supporting Actress.

"*Peyton Place* is an interminable survey of a New England town populated by a lot of dull people....it is woefully diffuse, and before it's over—roughly, three hours— boredom has set in like the grippe" —John McCarten, *New Yorker*, December 21, 1957

Pretty Woman ————————————————————
1990

> DIRECTOR: Garry Marshall; SCREENPLAY: J. F. Lawton; CAST:
> Richard Gere, Julia Roberts, Ralph Bellamy, Jason
> Alexander, Laura San Giacomo.
> One of the top five box-office hits of 1990. Academy
> Award nomination for Best Actress.

"...revoltingly boorish..." —Gary Giddins, *Village Voice*, March 27, 1990

"What's wrong with this picture is that it's an astonishingly self-oblivious piece of woman-bashing.... It's almost as if Disney is packaging a new theme park attraction—Hooker World.... What are we to make of the spectacle of a studio molding another beauty even more imperiously into a figure of gorgeous powerlessness? At best, *Pretty Woman* is condescending. It's a misogynist's delight." —Jay Carr, *Boston Globe*, March 23, 1990

"...blandly predictable, formulaic fare... The movie is so slick and so eager-to-please that both its queasy subtext and its message—a weird combination between anti- and pro-materialism (vast wealth is fine, but don't get *too* greedy)—likely will roll off the back of the white middle-class audience at which it's aimed. Which makes the whole enterprise all the more odious, all the more depressing." —David Kronke, *Dallas Times Herald*, March 23, 1990

Raiders of the Lost Ark ————————————
1981

> DIRECTOR: Steven Spielberg; SCREENPLAY: Lawrence Kasdan;
> CAST: Harrison Ford, Karen Allen, Denholm Elliott.
> One of the top ten box-office hits of all time.

"...confusing, ultimately piddling entertainment. *Raiders* tells us less about society as a whole, I'm afraid, than about Hollywood, which of late seems to be laboring under the illusion that today's moviegoers are subliterate teen-agers unable to distinguish between good and bad comic books. Or worse, perhaps films are now made by people who are no brighter than the dullest members of the audience they have in mind." —Robert Asahina, *New Leader,* June 29, 1981

"I don't myself find that a host of snakes will restore drama to a sagging thriller, but I must tell you that I've never seen a more determinded attempt to do so. Serpentine central casting must have been worked to a frazzle....After the escape from entombment and the cobras and asps, the film is simply a bore....So save your money." —Christopher Hitchens, *New Statesman,* July 31, 1981

Rain Man
1988

> DIRECTOR: Barry Levinson; SCREENPLAY: Ronald Bass, Barry Morrow; CAST: Dustin Hoffman, Tom Cruise, Valeria Golino.
>
> One of the top five box-office hits of 1988. Academy Award winner for Best Picture, Director, Original Screenplay, Actor (Dustin Hoffman); nominations for Best Score, Cinematography, Editing, Art Direction.

"...a sentimental contrivance, a buddies-on-the-road movie with yet another pair of opposites fumbling their way toward affection. Harmless as it is, it's bland and noncommittal, and it doesn't have much reason for being—apart from the fact that someone wanted to build a film around the autistic-savant syndrome....The

script is so blah that it seems almost paint-by-num-
bers." —David Edelstein, *New York Post,* December 16,
1988

Rebecca ————————————————————————
1940

> DIRECTOR: Alfred Hitchcock; SCREENPLAY: Robert E.
> Sherwood, Joan Harrison, adaptation by Phillip MacDonald
> and Michael Hogan from the novel by Daphne Du Maurier;
> CAST: Laurence Olivier, Joan Fontaine, George Sanders,
> Judith Anderson, Nigel Bruce, Reginald Denny, C. Aubrey
> Smith, Gladys Cooper.
>
> One of the top five box-office hits of 1940. Academy
> Award winner for Best Picture, Cinematography;
> nominations for Best Actor, Actress, Director, Score,
> Screenplay, Supporting Actress, Film Editing.

"Dave Selznick's picture is too tragic and deeply psychological to hit the fancy of wide audience appeal....General audiences will tab it as a long-drawn out
drama that could have been told better in less
footage." —*Variety,* March 27, 1940

Rocky ————————————————————————
1976

> DIRECTOR: John G. Avildsen; SCREENPLAY: Sylvester Stallone;
> CAST: Sylvester Stallone, Burgess Meredith, Talia Shire, Burt
> Young, Carl Weathers.
>
> Top box-office hit of 1976. Academy Award winner for
> Best Picture, Director; nominations for Best Actor,
> Supporting Actor, Supporting Actress, Screenplay, Song.

"*Rocky* is a textbook example of an overly grandiose script, performed with relentless grandiloquence. And when you can't hear and see Stallone trying too hard, director John Avildsen can be discerned puffing and posturing off camera.... Up to a point I'm willing to overlook the egg on a guy's face, but, really, there's such a thing as too much—especially when they're promoting this bloated, pseudo-epic as a low-budget Oscar-bound winner." —*Washington Star*, December 21, 1976

Saturday Night Fever
1977

> DIRECTOR: John Badham; SCREENPLAY: Norman Wexler, from a story by Nik Cohn; CAST: John Travolta, Karen Lynn Gorney, Barry Miller, Joseph Cali, Paul Pape, Bruce Ornstein, Donna Pescow.
>
> One of the top five box-office hits of 1977. Academy Award nomination for Best Actor (John Travolta).

"...a flagrantly foul-mouthed script and coarse viewpoint...*Fever* is a rabid variation on a theme that customarily evokes pathos—the loss of adolescent illusions and self-deceptions....one wouldn't have expected something this brutal and garish from the director of *Bingo Long*." —Gary Arnold, *Washington Post*, December 16, 1977

"*Saturday Night Fever* is nothing more than an updated '70s version of the Sam Katzman rock music cheapies of the '50s. That is to say, Robert Stigwood's production is a more shrill, more vulgar, more trifling, more superficial and more pretentious exploitation film...a major disappointment." —*Variety*, December 14, 1977

Sayonara
1957

DIRECTOR: Joshua Logan; SCREENPLAY: Paul Osborn, from
the novel by James Michener; CAST: Marlon Brando, Miyoshi
Umeki, Miiko Taka, Red Buttons, Ricardo Montalban.
   One of the top five box-office hits of 1957. Academy
Award winner for Best Supporting Actress (Miyoshi Umeki),
Supporting Actor (Red Buttons), Art Direction; nominations
for Best Picture, Screenplay, Director, Cinematography,
Actor, Editing.

"The amateur intellectualism of all this is not relieved by
amateur bits of Kabuki, flurries of even more amateurish
puppetry, and blobs of jiggling Japanese chorines, sprin-
kled throughout this faltering film by a patently worried
director." —Ellen Fitzpatrick, *Films in Review,*
December 1957

Shampoo
1975

DIRECTOR: Hal Ashby; SCREENPLAY: Robert Towne, Warren
Beatty; CAST: Warren Beatty, Julie Christie, Goldie Hawn,
Lee Grant, Jack Warden, Carrie Fisher.
   One of the top five box-office hits of 1975. Academy
Award for Best Supporting Actress (Lee Grant);
nominations for Best Screenplay, Supporting Actor.

"...an unlikable romp, neither edifying nor entertaining...It is, in fact, a conventional and hollow spectacle
decked sadly out in dirty words and shadowy sex
play." —David Sterritt, *Christian Science Monitor,* March
7, 1975

"*Shampoo* just doesn't wash very well...a mixed farcical
achievement which is beneath the proven talents of all

principal players as well as those of director Hal Ashby, star-producer-coscripter Warren Beatty, and writer Robert Towne....Lord, what a waste." —*Murf., Variety,* February 12, 1975

The Silence of the Lambs
1990

> DIRECTOR: Jonathan Demme; SCREENPLAY: Ted Tally, from the novel by Thomas Harris; CAST: Jodie Foster, Anthony Hopkins, Scott Glenn, Ted Levine, Anthony Heald.
> One of the top five box-office hits of 1991. Academy Award nominations for Best Picture, Director, Actor, Actress, Screenplay, Editing.

"For a change, a contemporary American movie actually does what it sets out to do. I suppose I should feel encouraged—but I don't. I'm dismayed that people should mistake competence for art, appalled that critics and audiences seem ready to wink at gay-bashing. And I'm disheartened that Jonathan Demme, whose best work has been so alert, so open to the way Americans live, would cocoon himself in this preposterous fantasy." —Stuart Klawans, *Nation,* February 25, 1991

The Snows of Kilimanjaro
1952

> DIRECTOR: Henry King; SCREENPLAY: Casey Robinson, from a story by Ernest Hemingway; CAST: Gregory Peck, Susan Hayward, Ava Gardner, Hildegard Neff, Leo G. Carroll.
> One of the top five box-office hits of 1954.

The Snows of Kilimanjaro is likely to remind most adult males of their more lurid adolescent daydreams....the movie is a Technicolor travelogue that ranges from

Africa to Europe to backwoods Michigan, a sort of scenic railway running through a Tunnel of Love...The acting honors are easily captured by a herd of hippopotami plunging like dolphins in an African river, and by a Hollywood hyena." —*Time*, September 22, 1952

The Song of Bernadette
1943

DIRECTOR: Henry King; SCREENPLAY: George Seaton, from the novel by Franz Werfel; CAST: Jennifer Jones, William Eythe, Charles Bickford, Vincent Price, Lee J. Cobb, Gladys Cooper.

One of the top five box-office hits of 1943. Academy Award winner for Best Actress (Jennifer Jones), Art Direction, Cinematography, Score; nominations for Best Picture, Screenplay, Director, Supporting Actress, Supporting Actor, Editing.

"*The Song of Bernadette* is an overwhelmingly careful failure....The script...is uninspired to the point of tedium....It is so cautious that near the end the whole production appears to be turning to stone; when people bend they creak, lifetime associates meet and come together with all of the recognition of ambulating sculptures, and they look at each other with paralyzed faces. It is actually one of the most sick, wracked films I have ever seen." —Manny Farber, *New Republic*, March 6, 1944

The Sound of Music
1965

DIRECTOR: Robert Wise; SCREENPLAY: Ernest Lehman; CAST: Julie Andrews, Christopher Plummer, Richard Haydn, Eleanor Parker, Peggy Wood.

Top box-office hit of 1965. Academy Award winner for
Best Picture, Director; nominations for Cinematography,
Actress, Supporting Actress.

"...pure unadulterated kitsch, not a false note, not a
whiff of reality; and every detail so carefully worked out,
all moving along so smoothly in the familiar tracks,
sparing one the slightest effort, all the seeing and feeling
and hearing done for one by competent, highly paid
professionals..." —Dwight Macdonald, *Esquire*, August
1966

"The movie is for the five-to-seven set and their mom-
mies who think their kids aren't up to the stinging
sophistication and biting wit of *Mary Poppins*—and who
can sit still for hours on end...." —Judith Crist, from
her collection *The Private Eye, the Cowboy and the Very
Naked Girl*, 1968

Spartacus
1960

DIRECTOR: Stanley Kubrick; SCREENPLAY: Dalton Trumbo,
from the novel by Howard Fast; CAST: Kirk Douglas,
Laurence Olivier, Charles Laughton, Tony Curtis, Jean
Simmons, Peter Ustinov, John Gavin.

One of the top five box-office hits of 1960. Academy
Award for Best Cinematography, Supporting Actor (Peter
Ustinov), Art Direction; nominations for Score, Editing.

"...bursting with patriotic fervor, bloody tragedy, a lot of
romantic fiddle-faddle and historical inaccuracy. Also, it
is pitched about to the level of a lusty schoolboy's
taste....Apparently, too many people, too many cooks
had their ladles in this stew, and it comes out a romantic

mish-mash." —Bosley Crowther, *New York Times*, October 7, 1960

Star Wars
1977

DIRECTOR: George Lucas; SCREENPLAY: George Lucas; CAST: Mark Hamill, Harrison Ford, Carrie Fisher, Peter Cushing, Alec Guinness, Anthony Daniels, Kenny Baker, David Prowse, Peter Mayhew.

One of the top five box-office hits of all time. Selected to the National Film Registry, Library of Congress. Academy Award winner for Best Score, Editing; nominations for Best Director, Picture, Screenplay, Supporting Actor. Winner of the British Academy of Film and Television Arts and Golden Globe awards for Best Score; Los Angeles Film Critics Association award for Best Picture.

"...about the dialogue there's nothing to be said. In fact the dialogue itself can hardly be said: it sticks in the actors' mouths like peanut butter. The acting is the School of Buster Crabbe, except for Alec Guinness, who mumbles through on the way to his salary check.... The only way that *Star Wars* could have been exciting was through its visual imagination and special effects. Both are unexceptional." —Stanley Kauffmann, *New Republic*, June 18, 1977

"O dull new world!...it is all as exciting as last year's weather reports...it is all trite characters and paltry verbiage, handled adequately by Harrison Ford...uninspiredly by Mark Hamill...and wretchedly by Carrie Fisher, who is not even appealing as Princess Leia Organa (an organic lay)...Still, *Star Wars* will do very

Harrison Ford and Mark Hamill in *Star Wars*

nicely for those lucky enough to be children or unlucky enough never to have grown up." —John Simon, *New York,* June 20, 1977

"The reviewer's lot is not an easy one and, at the risk of sounding like myself as a prissy 14-year-old, dammit, *Star Wars* is childish, even for a cartoon." —Molly Haskell, *Village Voice,* June 13, 1977

The Ten Commandments
1956

> DIRECTOR: Cecil B. De Mille; SCREENPLAY: Aeneas Mackenzie, Jesse L. Lasky Jr., Jack Gariss, Frederic M. Frank; CAST: Charlton Heston, Yul Brynner, Edward G. Robinson, Anne Baxter.
>
> Top box-office hit of 1955. Academy Award nominations for Best Picture, Cinematography, Art Direction, Editing.

"...the biggest, the most expensive, and in some respects perhaps the most vulgar movie ever made...roughly comparable to an eight-foot chorus girl—pretty well put together, but much too big and much too flashy."
—*Time*, November 12, 1956

"The idea—a romantic screen biography of Moses—is inherently ludicrous and irreverent, and the producer-director, himself something of a legend, has exercised a heroic bad taste to create an epic of balderdash."
—Robert Hatch, *Nation*, December 8, 1956

"If the movie of *War and Peace* is longer than the book, *The Ten Commandments* is longer than the 40 years in the desert. I left the theatre with bed-sores....Anyone with a nostalgic feeling for the De Mille badness of the past will be sorry that this film, which may be the last of its genre from the master, had to be such an utter catastrophe...." —Robert Evett, *New Republic*, December 10, 1956

Tom Jones
1963

> DIRECTOR: Tony Richardson; SCREENPLAY: John Osborne, from the novel by Henry Fielding; CAST: Albert Finney, Susannah York, Hugh Griffith, Edith Evans, Joan Greenwood, Diane Cilento, Joyce Redman.

One of the top five box-office hits of 1963. Academy
Award winner for Best Picture, Screenplay, Director, Score;
nominations for Best Actor, Supporting Actor. Winner of
the British Academy of Film and Television Arts awards for
Best Film, Screenplay, Supporting Actress, Art Direction.

"Richardson vulgarizes Fielding down to the level of a
road company production of *The Drunkard* until even
Dame Edith Evans begins to sound like Marjorie Main
essaying *The Importance of Being Earnest* for the Sioux Falls
Stock Company." —Andrew Sarris, *Village Voice,*
October 24, 1963

The Towering Inferno
1974

DIRECTOR: John Guillermin, Irwin Allen; SCREENPLAY:
Stirling Silliphant; CAST: Paul Newman, Steve McQueen,
William Holden, Faye Dunaway, Fred Astaire, Susan Blakely,
Richard Chamberlain.

Top box-office hit of 1974. Academy Award winner for
Cinematography, Song; nominations for Best Picture, Score,
Supporting Actor (Fred Astaire).

"At the end of the film, after the last flame has been
doused, Paul Newman surveys the ruined hulk of his
skyscraper. He suggests allowing it to stand as 'a monument to all the bullshit of our age.' Probably *The Towering
Inferno* should be placed on permanent exhibition at the
Smithsonian for the same reason." —Richard Schickel,
Time, January 6, 1975

The Untouchables
1987

DIRECTOR: Brian De Palma; SCREENPLAY: David Mamet;
CAST: Kevin Costner, Sean Connery, Robert De Niro,
Charles Martin Smith, Andy Garcia.

One of the top five box-office hits of 1987. Academy
Award winner for Best Supporting Actor (Sean Connery);
nominations for Score, Art Direction, Costume Design.

"On paper the combination of De Palma and Mamet
might sound promising, but in practice it's not.... all they
have added to their pop material...is seriousness, and it's
a dead weight around the movie's neck...the stakeout at
the train station here may be his greatest stunt yet...It's
stunning but in the way that great jugglers or magicians
can sometimes be stunning. But it's not art, and, at least
in the case of *The Untouchables*, it's only marginally
entertaining." —Hal Hinson, *Washington Post*, June 3,
1987

The Way We Were
1973

DIRECTOR: Sydney Pollack; SCREENPLAY: Arthur Laurents,
from his novel; CAST: Barbra Streisand, Robert Redford,
Patrick O'Neal, Viveca Lindfors, Bradford Dillman.
    One of the top five box-office hits of 1973. Academy
Award winner for Best Score; nominations for
Cinematography, Best Actress.

"Can you see Barbra Streisand as a frizzy-haired, radical,
creative-writing student at a northeastern university in
the year 1937? You can see her, all right, in a flabby,
reminiscent, nostalgic film called *The Way We Were*, but
somehow you don't believe her....What it ends up being
is one more attempt to ride the nostalgia wave—and one
more soppy, sappy, romanticized vehicle for superstar
Streisand." —Hollis Alpert, *Saturday Review/World*,
November 6, 1973

West Side Story
1961

> DIRECTOR: Robert Wise, Jerome Robbins; SCREENPLAY:
> Ernest Lehman; CAST: Natalie Wood, Richard Beymer, Russ
> Tamblyn, Rita Moreno, George Chakiris.
> One of the top five box-office hits of 1961. Academy
> Award winner for Best Picture, Director, Cinematography,
> Supporting Actress (Rita Moreno), Supporting Actor
> (George Chakiris), Musical Direction, Art Direction, Sound,
> Costume; nomination for Best Screenplay.

"How can so many critics have fallen for all this frenzied hokum?... I would guess that in a few decades the dances in *West Side Story* will look as much like hilariously limited, dated period pieces as Busby Berkeley's 'Remember the Forgotten Man' number in *Gold Diggers of 1933.*" —Pauline Kael, *Film Quarterly*, Summer 1962

White Christmas
1954

> DIRECTOR: Michael Curtiz; SCREENPLAY: Norman Krasna,
> Norman Panama, Melvin Frank; CAST: Bing Crosby, Danny
> Kaye, Rosemary Clooney, Vera-Ellen.
> Top box-office hit of 1954.

"You can safely take the youngsters or your mid-Victorian aunt, but I don't guarantee that they won't go to sleep." —Moira Walsh, *America*, November 6, 1954

3

Who Knew? Certainly Not the Critics!

Bad Early Reviews of Future Stars

Woody Allen
Bananas, 1971

"*Bananas* is full of hilarious comic ideas and lines, supplied by Allen and his collaborator Mickey Rose; then Allen, the director and actor, murders them....see Allen trapped on an exercise machine or at a trial where he is both lawyer and witness, and you'll see the quintessence of Amateur Night. He confuses the ability to write comedy with the ability to perform it. His directing is worse....On the rocks of his acting and direction *Bananas* splits." —Stanley Kauffmann, *New Republic,* May 22, 1971

"The fact is that intellectuals do not moonlight as stand-up comedians, and those who do have intellects that won't stand up. But a creeping pretentiousness spreads over their material, and pretty soon they are full of unfunny jokes about Kierkegaard and such, and instead of slipping on banana peels, they are making political satires about banana republics without knowing beans about their politics." —John Simon, from his collection *Reverse Angle,* 1982.

Lauren Bacall
Confidential Agent, 1945

"The Bacall publicity has plainly pushed the young woman too far too fast. Neither a great beauty nor a great actress, her voice and facial expressions, both limited, soon grow monotonous. She is not even the interesting personality which careful direction made of her in *To Have and Have Not.*" —*Time,* November 19, 1945

The Big Sleep, 1946

"Miss Bacall is a dangerous-looking female, but she still hasn't learned to act." —Bosley Crowther, *New York Times,* August 24, 1946

Brigitte Bardot
And God Created Woman, 1957

"A brouhaha in a bias cup...In promulgating Brigitte as a full-blown enchantress, the French have clearly sent a girl to do a woman's job." —*Time,* November 11, 1957

Warren Beatty
Splendor in the Grass, 1961

"I am told Hollywood hopes to make him a star, but his face, at least in this picture, is on the weak side, and doesn't always photograph well." —*Films in Review,* November 1961

Jean-Paul Belmondo
Breathless, 1959

"A hypnotically ugly new young man...The most effective cigarette-mouther and thumb-to-lip rubber since time began." —Bosley Crowther, *New York Times*, February 8, 1961

Ingrid Bergman
Intermezzo, 1939

"...a rather over-heated Hepburn..." —John Mosher, *New Yorker*, October 7, 1939

Gary Cooper
A Farewell to Arms, 1932

"He is an innocuous young man, who at least looks and acts like a man; but he is first and last a movie actor, that is to say, no actor at all." —Pare Lorentz, *Vanity Fair*, January 1933

Francis Ford Coppola
You're a Big Boy Now, 1967

"While everyone was busy turning each other on, no one remembered to ask Mr. Coppola if, in fact, he actually had a personal statement to make or a personal style in which to make it. He does not." —Richard Schickel, *Life*, March 24, 1967

The Rain People, 1969

"In this as in the other four feature films he has directed...Coppola reveals only a fine sense of technique. And while technique is sufficient for musical and horror films, it is not sufficient for a film that aims to be character study.... What Coppola needed was someone who could work out a good screenplay with him. His past efforts as a script writer have shown little talent. —Jerry De Muth, *Christian Century*, December 31, 1969

Tom Cruise
Risky Business, 1983

"...a standard-issue baby-faced actor..." —David Denby, *New York*, August 22, 1983

"The boy, Tom Cruise, isn't very appealing." —Stanley Kauffmann, *New Republic*, September 19 & 26, 1983

Beverly D'Angelo
Hair, 1979

"Forman has cast as Sheila, the upper-class heroine whose conversion to hippiedom is the crux of the tale, Beverly D'Angelo, whose lack of talent, charm, looks, and hauteur is such that she could no more pass for upper-crust than a camel for the thread in a needle's eye." —John Simon, from his collection *Reverse Angle*, 1982

Doris Day
Romance on the High Seas, 1948

"...it is hard to work up enthusiasm for the Warners' new starlet, Doris Day. Maybe this bouncy young lady...has ability and personality. But as shown in this picture...she has no more than a vigorous disposition which hits the screen with a thud." —Bosley Crowther, *New York Times*, June 26, 1948

James Dean

East of Eden, 1955
Academy Award nomination for Best Actor.

"Kazan has apparently attempted to graft a Brando-type personality and set of mannerisms upon Dean, and the result is less than successful.... this artful construction of a performance is not, to get Stanislavskian about it, building a character." —Lee Rogow, *Saturday Review,* March 19, 1955

"It is the acting that will really get you down. We can begin with the performance of a youth called James Dean.... He looks like a sort of miniature Gregory Peck, but he has obviously been going to a few movies featuring Marlon Brando....Sometimes he jumps up and down like a kangaroo, sometimes he giggles like a lunatic, and sometimes he is surly and offended. He's a hard man to decipher." —John McCarten, *New Yorker,* March 19, 1955

Giant, 1956
Academy Award nomination for Best Actor.

"Dean made the young Jett Rink such a boor not even a wife more neurotic than the one Miss Taylor was portraying could have thought him attractive. Since Dean is dead I shall say nothing about his attempt to portray the mature Jett Rink, except to say it is embarrassing to see." —Courtland Phipps, *Films in Review,* November 1956

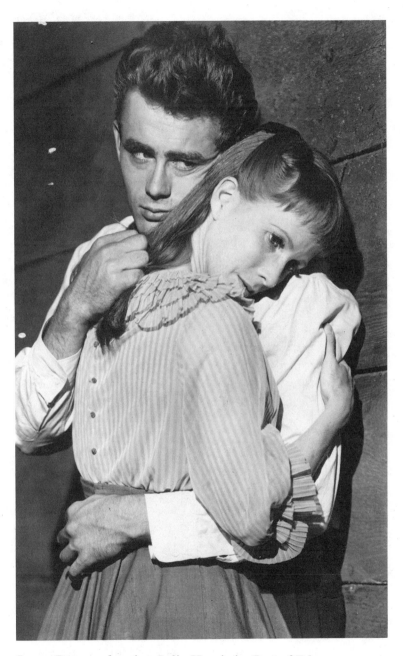

James Dean embracing Julie Harris in *East of Eden*

Jonathan Demme _____
Melvin and Howard, 1980

"The situation in film criticism is becoming much like that in theater criticism: any American who shows the slightest wisp of talent, who is not utterly hopeless, gets wheeled right up to the pumping station for inflation....In film it's directors, this week's example being Jonathan Demme." —Stanley Kauffmann, *New Republic,* November 8, 1980

Robert De Niro _____
Greetings, 1968

"Of...Robert De Niro and Jonathan Warden, the latter gives at least some evidence of a little talent." —Howard Thompson, *New York Times,* December 16, 1968

Catherine Deneuve _____
Repulsion, 1965

"As the homicidal zombie, Catherine Deneuve plays her role to the hilt, which is, unfortunately, a boring thing to watch." —Brendan Gill, *New Yorker,* October 9, 1965

Jodie Foster _____
Taxi Driver, 1976
   Academy Award nomination for Best Supporting Actress;
   winner of the British Academy of Film and Televisions Arts
   award for Best Supporting Actress.

"Jodie Foster as the 12-year-old is only minimally effective." —Stanley Kauffmann, *New Republic,* March 6, 1976

Jean-Luc Godard
Breathless, 1960

"Godard's directorial abilities seem to me to be rather flash-in-the-pan-ish. He lacks intellectual and artistic integrity." —H. H., *Films in Review,* March 1961

Charles Grodin
The Heartbreak Kid, 1972

"...a young man on his honeymoon is attracted by another girl...(He is played by Charles Grodin in stock metropolitan-Jew revue-sketch manner.)"—Stanley Kauffmann, *New Republic,* January 6 & 13, 1973

Goldie Hawn
Cactus Flower, 1969
   Academy Award and Golden Globe winner for Best
   Supporting Actress.

"...a listless little chickadee from *Laugh-In,* who plays Matthau's mistress like an illustration for a bird-seed commercial. Maybe those wide-eyed one-liners and pregnant pauses work on television, but if Miss Hawn is to have any kind of future in movies, she needs to learn something about the rudimentary techniques necessary to sustain a comic scene without putting the audience to sleep." —Rex Reed, *Holiday,* November 1969

Katharine Hepburn
Christopher Strong, 1933

"The role of the daughter in *A Bill of Divorcement* is evidently a fool-proof one.... A few months past movie audiences were sure that a new star had come into their firmament when they saw Katharine Hepburn essay the part...but in *Christopher Strong* Miss Hepburn does little to show that she has earned the star rating that her producers have accorded her.... The cinema critic of the *London Observer,* Miss C. A. Lejeune, winced at Miss Hepburn's voice in *A Bill of Divorcement.* As Al Jolson would say, 'she ain't heard nothin' yet.'"   —*Newsweek,* March 18, 1933

Dustin Hoffman
The Graduate, 1967
   Academy Award nomination for Best Actor.

"*The Graduate* is a genuinely funny comedy which succeeds in being so despite an uninteresting and untalented actor in the title role."   —Adelaide Comerford, *Films in Review,* January 1968

Carol Kane
Hester Street, 1975
   Academy Award nomination for Best Actress.

"You have to have a stomach for ugliness to endure the face of Carol Kane—to say nothing of the zombielike expressions she mistakes for acting."   —John Simon, *New York,* October 20, 1975

Lawrence Kasdan
Body Heat, 1981

"Kasdan calls himself a writer. Moreover, in interviews and on talk shows he has been self-righteously condemning the ill-treatment he and his colleagues receive in Hollywood. From the evidence in *Body Heat*, in his case that treatment is clearly deserved. The only real question is why things seem to have gotten better for him." —Robert Asahina, *New Leader*, September 21, 1981

Continental Divide, 1981

"Lawrence Kasdan appears to have grown up inside a television tube (there isn't a hint of real experience in anything he's written), but I'm not sure he's understood even what he's seen there." —David Denby, *New York*, September 28, 1981

Marilyn Monroe
Don't Bother to Knock, 1952

"...unfortunately, all the equipment that Miss Monroe has to handle the job are a childishly blank expression and a provokingly feeble, hollow voice..." —Bosley Crowther, *New York Times*, July 19, 1952

Paul Newman
The Silver Chalice, 1954

"Paul Newman, a lad who resembles Marlon Brando, delivers his lines with the emotional fervor of a Putnam Division conductor announcing local stops." —John McCarten, *New Yorker*, January 15, 1955

"...Paul Newman—a poor man's Marlon Brando..." —Kenneth Coyte, *Saturday Review*, January 15, 1955

Nick Nolte
The Deep, 1977

"With his attenuated forehead and befogged eyes, his prognathous and semicretinous aspect, he looks very much like one of those late and degenerate Hapsburg monarchs of Spain whom not even the brush of Velazquez could, or would, whitewash. Not only can he not act, he cannot even look and sound halfway intelligent during the rare moments when the screenplay calls for it." —John Simon, *New York,* July 4, 1977

Gregory Peck
Keys of the Kingdom, 1944
    Academy Award nomination for Best Actor.

"I wonder, too, why I thought Gregory Peck a particularly gifted actor. Now, it seems to me that he probably has talent, in a still semi-professional stage." —James Agee, *Nation,* January 6, 1945

Anthony Perkins
Friendly Persuasion, 1956
    Academy Award nomination for Best Supporting Actor.

"...The performance of Anthony Perkins...seemed to me a mistake Wyler should have avoided....some of his gambols and contortions were simply Strassbergian absurdities—not acting...his oddly composed face had an unpleasant, almost a mean semblance." —Diana Willing, *Films in Review,* November 1956

Elvis Presley ——————————————————
Love Me Tender, 1956

"...a young man of hulk and probably flabby muscle, with a degenerate face, who sings emasculated innuendoes in a southern drawl as he strums a guitar...The weak mouth seems to sneer, even in repose, and the large, heavily-lidded eyes, seem open only to be on the look-out for opportunities for self-indulgence. The long hair is one of today's badges of the psychologically feminized male....How a society as dynamic as our own throws up such a monstrosity is beyond the scope of this review." —Henry Hart, *Films in Review,* December 1956

Vanessa Redgrave ——————————————
Blow-Up, 1966

"The murderess (played with helpless annoyance by Vanessa Redgrave, like a lady caught in public with a hangnail and no emery board)..." —Rex Reed, from his collection *Big Screen, Little Screen,* 1971

Morgan!, 1966
   Academy Award nomination for Best Actress. Winner of the
   Best Actress prize at the Cannes Film Festival.

"I don't think...that Miss Redgrave, handsome as she is, is much of an actress, not here anyway; she seemed stiff, mechanical, trying to make up for an uneasiness about the meaning of her part (with which I sympathize) by violent contortions of her lovely face and limbs..."
—Dwight Macdonald, *Esquire,* October 1966

Eric Roberts
King of the Gypsies, 1978

"But Eric Roberts, where did they get *him?* A dynamo it needs; a dimwit dip it has got."   —Lawrence O'Toole, *Macleans,* December 25, 1978

"In the role of Dave, newcomer Eric Roberts looks and acts as if he were a cross between Robby Benson and Richard Gere, alternating strangled inarticulateness with fits of violence."   —Robert Asahina, *New Leader,* January 15, 1979

Jane Russell
The Outlaw, 1943

"Jane, as a sulky sexy, persistently semiclad halfbreed, had a relatively minor part. Critics would probably wonder whether the longest, lushest buildup in cinema history was worth it. Jane, who has privately professed a preference for interior decorating and home life (with her husband, pro football star Bob Waterfield), might at long last be allowed to try them out."   —*Time,* March 25, 1946

"This was the first picture in which the beauteous Jane Russell appeared and, while she is undeniably decorative in low-cut blouses, she is hopelessly inept as an actress."   —E. J. B., *New York Times,* September 12, 1947

The Paleface, 1948

"Miss Russell, while blessed by nature with certain well-advertised charms, appears to be lacking completely a modest ability to act. And although that is not very serious, so far as fan favor is concerned, it does limit somewhat the deference which Miss Russell might hope to command." —Bosley Crowther, *New York Times*, December 16, 1948

John Schlesinger
Billy Liar, 1963

"Schlesinger is obviously a man to watch for future awards. Everything he does is so wrong that the accumulation of errors resembles a personal style." —Andrew Sarris, *Village Voice*, December 19, 1963

Steven Spielberg
The Sugarland Express, 1974

"If we compare *Badlands* with *The Sugarland Express*, the difference between the artist and the mere smartass becomes overwhelmingly manifest." —John Simon, *Esquire,* June 1974

Jaws, 1975

"The direction is by Steven Spielberg, who did the unbearable *Sugarland Express*. At least here he has shucked most of his arty mannerisms and has progressed almost to the level of a stock director of the '30s—say, Roy del Ruth." —Stanley Kauffmann, *New Republic,* July 26, 1975

John Travolta
Saturday Night Fever, 1977
Academy Award nomination for Best Actor.

"...at no time are we watching a young man who demonstrates a natural or exciting flair for dancing...one heard a lot of drivel about how hard Travolta

worked to perfect his uninspired strutting and preening and hand-jiving…It remains to be seen what the picture may do to or for John Travolta. I have grave doubts about the romantic potential of a young actor whose most appealing expression is a kind of dumb vulnerability—Brian De Palma seemed to have the right idea when he cast Travolta as a stooge in *Carrie*."
—Gary Arnold, *Washington Post*, December 16, 1977

Kathleen Turner
Body Heat, 1981

"A shady lady, Matty Walker (played by a wooden-faced nonentity named Kathleen Turner)…" —Robert Asahina, *New Leader*, September 21, 1981

Lana Turner
The Postman Always Rings Twice, 1946

"I don't think any actress registers the wrong way as constantly as Lana Turner. Since MGM is determined to make a star of her, I wish they would let her go into a movie without the Arabian Nights decoration job, and put her in a part that calls for loyalty, friendliness and lower-middle-class respectability." —Manny Farber, *New Republic*, May 20, 1946

Susannah York
Tunes of Glory, 1960

"Newcomer Susannah York struck me as a starlet who is unlikely to burgeon into a star." —Ellen Fitzpatrick, *Films in Review*, January 1961

4

Shooting Stars _____

Critical Potshots at Major Talents

Woody Allen _____
Sleeper, 1973

"The source of Allen's popularity has always escaped me; I find him a very thin slice of Harold Lloyd on rye." — Robert Hatch, *Nation,* January 5, 1974

"To be sure *Sleeper* does display a growing dexterity at slapstick, and provides perhaps the first occasion in his films (his cruising dopily in a wheelchair near the beginning) when I can actually recall him and not the lines as what was funny. Given that rate of progress toward comic charisma, Woody Allen might just inch his way past the Three Stooges by the year 2000....one wonders if the effort is worth it." —William S. Pechter, *Commentary,* May 1974

Robert Altman _____
Brewster McCloud, 1970

"...directed in the style of Myra Breckinridge (hysterical confusion) by Robert Altman, who, I find difficult to admit, also directed *M*A*S*H*. Another mess like this, and he may be forced to retire early—not only from movies but from sane society as well." —Rex Reed, *Holiday*, August 1969

McCabe & Mrs. Miller, 1971

"The cinematic incompetence of director-scripter Robert Altman is all too visible in this immature farrago." —*Films in Review*, August/September 1971

Thieves Like Us, 1974

"Altman has most of the qualifications for a major director except the supreme one of having something significant to say." —John Simon, *Esquire*, May 1974

Ann-Margret
Carnal Knowledge, 1971
   Academy Award nomination for Best Supporting Actress.
   Golden Globe winner for Best Supporting Actress.

"It is Ann-Margret, as Bobbie, who is being hailed as the acting find of the movie.... True, there are those pitiful exposures of a famous body going to seed.... We see the pushed-up breasts.... We get low-angle shots turning the naked buttocks into medicine balls.... And we see the slightly sagging face, in relentless close-up, looking worried while trying to seduce. But something is lacking; a performance. Ann-Margret provides little more than the bulbous shell; missing are the quivering insides." —John Simon, *New Leader*, August 9, 1971

Alan Bates
Zorba the Greek, 1964

"He stands around dumbly, like a prop mistakenly left over from another movie." —Elizabeth Hardwick, *Vogue,* February 15, 1965

Candice Bergen
Carnal Knowledge, 1971

"Miss Bergen cannot act any age even though, with every new film, she tries harder, which does make her a *rara avis* among no-talent actresses." —John Simon, *New Leader,* August 9, 1971

Ingmar Bergman
The Virgin Spring, 1959
Academy Award winner for Best Foreign Film.

"...he could make great films. Instead, he thinks anything he hurries to the screen will be accepted. This lack of professional integrity is causing the discerning to withdraw their good will. Once they do so completely, the vogue-chasers will forsake Bergman, and so, thereafter, will the public he has never taken the trouble to serve—by making a *finished* film." —Helen Weldon Kuhn, *Films in Review,* November 1960

Busby Berkeley
42nd Street, 1933

"Busby Berkeley, the dance director, has gone to a lot of ineffectual bother about his intricate formations, not having been told that masses of chorus girls mean something only in the flesh. His talent is wasted in the films." —*Newsweek*, March 18, 1933

Leonard Bernstein
West Side Story, 1962

"Bernstein's music is pastiche; one hears echoes of Rodgers, Kern, Porter, even Romberg, even Stravinsky, for Mr. Bernstein is very *au courant*, a great hand at orchestration, but there's little to orchestrate." —Dwight MacDonald, *Esquire*, February 1962

Jacqueline Bisset
Day for Night, 1973

"...as usual, looking warm and beautiful and acting monotonously..." —Pauline Kael, *New Yorker*, October 15, 1973

Humphrey Bogart
Casablanca, 1942

"So tough that at one moment he looks like Buster Keaton playing Paul Gauguin." —*Time*, November 30, 1942

Marlon Brando
Sayonara, 1957
Academy Award nomination for Best Actor.

"He plays corn pone with West Point trimmings, and his speech has slumped to the point of pure novocaine....Also the weight he has put on gives him an occasional disconcerting resemblance to Alfred Hitchcock." —Robert Hatch, *Nation*, December 21, 1957

One-Eyed Jacks, 1961

"He plays the sleepy cat and the striking snake as though his forte were animal impersonations."
—Robert Hatch, *Nation*, April 15, 1961

The Chase, 1966

"Marlon Brando, who gave up acting shortly after *On the Waterfront*, is now simply a balding, middle-aged, potbellied man driven to undisciplined excesses that are clearly inexcusable on the screen....Most of the time he sounds like he has a mouth full of wet toilet paper."
—Rex Reed, from his collection *Big Screen, Little Screen*, 1971

The Godfather, 1972
Academy Award and Golden Globe winner for Best Actor.

"The acting is predominantly good, with the exception of the highly touted and critically acclaimed performance of Marlon Brando in the title part. Brando has a weak, gray voice, a poor ear for accents, and an unrivaled capacity for hamming things up by sheer underacting—in particular by unconscionably drawn-out pauses." —John Simon, *New Leader*, May 1, 1972

Last Tango in Paris, 1972
Academy Award nomination for Best Actor.

"A perfomance that would be an affront from anyone else is considered 'princely' coming from Brando....He gives us a star turn in French and English, an anthology of all his best parts or, rather, highlights from them." —John Simon, *New Leader*, February 19, 1973

Richard Brooks
Sweet Bird of Youth, 1962

"Mr. Brooks has a considerable reputation, one of the many things I don't understand about movies." —Dwight Macdonald, *Esquire*, June 1962

Nicolas Cage
Raising Arizona, 1987

"Any picture that stars Nicolas Cage is off to a shaky start, and when Cage is supposed to be winsome, the shakes become tremors." —Stanley Kauffmann, *New Republic*, April 13, 1987

Michael Caine
Alfie, 1966
Academy Award nomination for Best Actor.

"Women in the audience may feel the excitement, but it seemed to me that Caine lacked the charm of subtlety and was sweating rather freely." —Robert Hatch, *Nation*, September 12, 1966

Art Carney
Harry and Tonto, 1974
Academy Award and Golden Globe winner for Best Actor.

"Art Carney's performance is inexpressive and dull enough to earn him an Oscar." —John Simon, *Esquire*, November 1974

Keith Carradine
Nashville, 1975

"The recent rise of Keith Carradine to something approaching star status sounds an ominous note for Western civilization.... There are a good many images whose repetition is not helping our civilization to become any less fragile, but a couple certainly stand out. One of these is Richard Nixon, sweating in close-ups, and the other is Keith Carradine, lying in bed with the covers up to his navel, dialing a telephone." —Larry McMurtry, *American Film,* July/August 1977

Pretty Baby, 1978

"With his sepulchral demeanor, he looks less like an obsessed artist than a constipated undertaker." —Frank Rich, *Time,* April 10, 1978

"The longest hank of ambulatory Jello ever to blobble past a camera." —Stanley Kauffmann, *New Republic,* April 15, 1978

"Keith Carradine confirms his histrionic pallor and monotony." —John Simon, *Macleans,* May 15, 1978

John Cassavetes
A Woman Under the Influence, 1974
Academy Award nomination for Best Director.

"Cerebration, though, is a downright impediment to the non-artist, a label that fits John Cassavetes as perfectly as a stretch sock.... Why did Cassavetes, who could act pretty decently, want to become a filmmaker? Upward mobility is a dangerous thing in an actor." —John Simon, *Esquire,* April 1975

"The curse of filmmaking, as John Cassavetes shows us yet again, is that it's too easy." —Stanley Kauffmann, *New Republic*, December 28, 1974

Chevy Chase
National Lampoon's Vacation, 1983

"Just how bad is Chase? Let's put it this way: You could label his performance Swift's Premium, and sell it by the pound." —Joe Leydon, *Houston Post,* July 29, 1983

"...There's just no excuse for Chevy Chase's work anymore. Assuming the man can read, he must have understood that this was a script with little value. Perhaps he has resigned himself to being the Jerry Lewis of the '90s, but if that's what he wants he'll have to improve. A lot." —Catharine Rambeau, *Detroit Free Press,* July 29, 1983

Julie Christie
Petulia, 1968

"Miss Christie's hair-do is hideous, and her non-acting is redeemed only twice by the quality that once was in her..." —Rachel Weisbrod, *Films in Review,* June/July 1968

McCabe & Mrs. Miller, 1971
  Academy Award nomination for Best Actress.

"The once promising Julie Christie is still worthy of better things than attempting, under Altman's witless supervision, to play a whore-madam the like of which was never seen in West or East." —*Films in Review,* August/September 1971

Montgomery Clift ───────────────────

From Here to Eternity, 1953
  Academy Award nomination for Best Actor.

"...casting oddities include: Montgomery Clift, who would have trouble staying in the ring with a Boy Scout, as the Army's former middle-weight champion..."
—Moira Walsh, *America,* August 15, 1953

Raintree County, 1957

"Montgomery Clift, talking through his nose and expressing sensitivity of soul by seldom looking other cast members in the eyes, jitters through the role of John Shawnessy." —*Time,* January 6, 1958

Freud, 1962

"...his acting technique consists of no more than a stare..." —Ellen Fitzpatrick, *Films in Review,* January 1963

Joan Crawford ───────────────────
Rain, 1932

"And as for the miscast Miss Crawford, she was very obviously out without her rubbers, and the dramatic waters were well above her shoe-tops." —Cy Caldwell, *New Outlook,* November 1932

Johnny Guitar, 1954

"As usual, smouldering away like a baffled volcano and occasionally erupting into a flood of molten cliches..."
—Virginia Graham, *Spectator,* June 4, 1954

Strait Jacket, 1964

"As for Pepsi-Cola Board Member Crawford, she plainly plays her mad scenes For Those Who Think Jung."
—*Time,* February 7, 1964

David Cronenberg
The Dead Zone, 1983

"Director David Cronenberg has made a name for himself in the horror movie realm with exploding heads in *Scanners* and strange stuff in *Videodrome,* but apparently the goodies offered up by a major studio and big budget have stunted his style into massive mediocrity.
—Roxanne T. Mueller, *Cleveland Plain Dealer,* October 24, 1983

"Cronenberg hasn't toned down his style—he has taken a vacation. It's difficult to believe he was actually awake when many of the tediously plodding scenes in *Dead Zone* were shot....maybe it's time for him to go back to exploding heads..." —Joe Leydon, *Houston Post,* October 22, 1983

Tom Cruise
Born on the Fourth of July, 1989
Academy Award nomination for Best Actor.

"How is Cruise? He rises to the occasion once or twice....But Cruise isn't a smart or imaginative enough actor to make Kovic's rabid patriotism more than a hollow pose." —David Edelstein, *New York Post,* December 20, 1989

Billy Crystal ————————————————————
City Slickers, 1991

"...a cinematic black hole as far as charm and screen charisma are concerned..." —Anne Billson, *New Statesman and Society*, October 18, 1991

Robert De Niro ————————————————
The King of Comedy, 1982

"De Niro cunningly puts in all the stupid little things that actors customarily leave out. It's a studied performance; De Niro has learned to be a total fool. Big accomplishment!...De Niro's performance—from the Nobody's-Home school of acting—is of a piece with Scorsese's whole conception of the film." —Pauline Kael, *New Yorker*, March 7, 1983

Raging Bull, 1980
    Academy Award, Golden Globe, and New York Film Critics Circle award for Best Actor.

"What De Niro does in this picture isn't acting, exactly, I'm not sure what it is. Though it may at some level be awesome, it definitely isn't pleasurable." —Pauline Kael, *New Yorker*, December 8, 1980

Marlene Dietrich ————————————————
Blonde Venus, 1932

"As complete an exhibition of somnambulance as any actress ever gave an enthusiastic, if misled, public." —Pare Lorentz, *Vanity Fair*, November 1932

"...walks through her part with all the warmth and quiet restraint of a poker leaning against the fireplace..." —Cy Caldwell, *New Outlook*, November 1932

The Scarlet Empress, 1934

"As for Miss Dietrich, who retains the identical bisque doll expression through half a hundred costumes, her performance is less an exhibition of acting than of mesmerism." —William Troy, *Nation*, October 3, 1934

"One of the great disappointments of the work is the performance of Miss Dietrich. As usual, she looks beautiful, but, particularly in the first half of the work, she goes about with a vacant smile which makes one suspect that Catherine was just as defective mentally as her mad husband, Czar Peter III." —*Literary Digest*, September 29, 1934

Matt Dillon
Rumblefish, 1983

"Matt Dillon gives his patented suffering-beauty, cocky-but-vulnerable performance; the bright promise he once exhibited in *Over the Edge* and *Tex* has receded into the sludge of his unappealing voice, sloppy technique, and humorless temperament." —David Denby, *New York*, October 31, 1983

Faye Dunaway
Network, 1976
    Academy Award winner for Best Actress.

"Miss Dunaway, playing the meanest woman to be seen in an American film since the Wicked Witch of the West, oversells the programming V.P.'s bitchiness so much it's hard to take her seriously. Her character is supposed to be television incarnate, we're told, but she's really *Network* incarnate: she's so busy trying to outrage us that she doesn't even notice that she's drowning in her own bile." —Frank Rich, *New York Post*, November 15, 1976

Mommie Dearest, 1981

"Dunaway does not chew scenery. Dunaway starts neatly at each corner of the set in every scene and swallows it whole, costars and all." —*Variety*, September 9, 1981

Clint Eastwood
Coogan's Bluff, 1968

"There is simply no hint of comedy in Eastwood's dead pan. He moves through it all talking in low monosyllables, getting beaten to a pulp (without lasting effect) and turning women on and off like light switches.... He is constantly being upstaged by more colorful minor characters." —Vincent Canby, *New York Times*, October 3, 1968

Kelley's Heroes, 1970

"Eastwood manages not to change expression once during the 149 minutes of this nonsense." —Judith Crist, *New York*, June 22, 1970

Every Which Way But Loose, 1978

"After about 15 minutes of Eastwood's mugging, I began to long for the implacable stoicism of Dirty Harry." —Robert Asahina, *New Leader*, January 15, 1979

The Unforgiven, 1992

"A prominent New York critic once declared Clint Eastwood 'the last serious man in Hollywood.'... Eastwood's a serious man, all right, but, unfortunately, seriousness without an equal portion of talent is a mixed blessing." —Hal Hinson, *Washington Post,* August 7, 1992

Peter Falk
A Woman Under the Influence, 1974

"Peter Falk acts devoted beyond the call of duty, expansive beyond the call of nature, and dogged beyond the call of the wild." —John Simon, *Esquire,* April 1975

"Peter Falk is the husband with his usual bag of tricks—self-conscious solidity, pauses, all the diamond-in-the-rough cliches." —Stanley Kauffmann, *New Republic,* December 28, 1974

Mia Farrow
Secret Ceremony, 1969

"Mia Farrow, I am convinced, is incapable of playing anything but demented creeps. The simplest gestures, like opening doors and saying 'Dinner is served,' defeat her." —Rex Reed, *Holiday,* January 1969

Federico Fellini
Amarcord, 1973
    Academy Award nomination for Best Director.

"Lacking the wit of a Swift or a Voltaire, the best Fellini can look forward to is equaling the dismal record of a

Ken Russell.... And to think that this once great artist is still only fifty-four, an age at which one hasn't even earned the right to the excuse of senility." —John Simon, from his collection *Something To Declare*, 1983

Albert Finney
Two for the Road, 1967

"For Albert Finney... I can say nothing good. His acting ability is still rudimentary and his animal magnetism is still disfigured by boorish over-compensations. I think women's only pleasure in watching him is the cruel one of thinking up ways to tie him in knots. I can't conceive of men liking to watch him." —Flavia Wharton, *Films in Review*, May 1967

Jane Fonda
Barbarella, 1968

"Miss Fonda's abilities are stretched to the breaking point along with her clothes." —*Variety*, October 9, 1968

Nine to Five, 1980

"Fonda's reputation as an empty-headed activist is sadly borne out here." —Robert Asahina, *New Leader*, December 29, 1980

"...she plays her character like a cross between Barbarella and Barbie doll..." —Richard Corliss, *Time*, December 22, 1980

Harrison Ford
Blade Runner, 1982

"By now it is hard to tell at what level of irony, if any, Harrison Ford is pushing his distinctively dyspeptic

John Phillip Law and Jane Fonda in *Barbarella*

personality across the screen." —Andrew Sarris, *Village Voice,* July 6, 1982

Milos Forman
Taking Off, 1971

"I consider Milos Forman morally deficient to the utmost degree, and, as usually though not always follows, a worthless imitation of an artist. And I think that the army of his admirers, whether critics or audiences, are, at the very least, dupes and fools." —John Simon, *New Leader,* May 3, 1971

Jodie Foster
The Silence of the Lambs, 1990
   Academy Award nomination for Best Actress.

"Her spare, peck-mouthed face is not a highly expressive actor's mask. Her acting choices, from moment to moment, always seem to come from an available stock.... Foster seems to have not much more than industrious application. She fills in the spaces allotted to her by the script, but she never provides more than the expected." —Stanley Kauffmann, *New Republic,* February 18, 1991

Clark Gable
Gone With the Wind, 1939
   Academy Award nomination for Best Actor.

"Clark Gable managed to be just the size ordered and to shift his gumdrop from side to side with unusual aplomb." —Otis Ferguson, *New Republic,* April 22, 1940

Teacher's Pet, 1958

"Mr. Gable looks and sounds a little too much like President Eisenhower." —Hollis Alpert, *Saturday Review*, March 22, 1958

Greta Garbo
Grand Hotel, 1932

"Our observations must also record the extremely pathetic Miss Garbo, before whose photograph countless American college boys have been offering up prayers these last ten years. For all her beautiful head and appealingly awkward lankiness, Miss Garbo steadily loses her spell through the sound machines. Speaking our language badly, she must be cast always as a foreigner, mumbling but a few words at a time, As usual she has the air of an aspirin addict; she still wears the perpetual headache which once seemed so intriguing in the deaf-and-dumb pictures." —Matthew Josephson, *New Republic*, April 27, 1932

Judy Garland
The Wizard of Oz, 1939

"It isn't that this little slip of a miss spoils the fantasy so much as that her thumping, overgrown gambols are characteristic of its treatment here: when she is merry the house shakes, and everybody gets wet when she is lorn." —Otis Ferguson, *New Republic*, September 20, 1939

Richard Gere
Pretty Woman, 1990

"Richard Gere has become the Sonny Tufts of his day. His every line is spoken in a flat monotone.... He has no timing, and he never, never focuses his beady little eyes on another actor." —Gary Giddins, *Village Voice*, March 27, 1990

Mel Gibson
Lethal Weapon, 1987

"The performance should make him a shoo-in for an honorary degree from the Rodney Dangerfield school of eye-bulging, nose-twitching histrionics. Trouble is, he didn't mean to be funny." —Johanna Steinmetz, *Chicago Tribune*, March 6, 1987

Jerry Goldsmith
The Omen, 1976
    Academy Award for Best Score.

"...Most annoying...is the music by that pretentious hack Jerry Goldsmith, who has cannibalized Stravinsky without crediting him." —John Simon, *New York*, July 12, 1976

Ruth Gordon
Rosemary's Baby, 1968
    Academy Award and Golden Globe winner for Supporting
    Actress.

"The lone authentic bit of horror in the film is Ruth Gordon's performance: a sort of self-serving, nonstop tuneless singsong issuing from a decrepit butterfly that thinks itself the Empress Theodora, it is easily one of the most offensive spectacles of any year and does make *Rosemary's Baby*, whenever it is on view, perhaps not horrifying but certainly disgusting." —John Simon, *New Leader*, July 8, 1968

Where's Poppa?, 1970

"Ruth Gordon is the mother, giving the same eccentric performance she has been giving for many, many years, except that now, mercifully, she doesn't try to be sexy." —Stanley Kauffmann, *New Republic*, December 5, 1970

Barbara Harris
Oh Dad, Poor Dad, Mama's Hung You in the Closet and I'm Feeling So Sad, 1966

"...much too fat to roll about on top of billiard tables in lace bikinis like a baby hippopotamus in diapers..." —Rex Reed, from his collection *Big Screen, Little Screen*, 1971

Laurence Harvey
Butterfield 8, 1960

"I am not among the ladies who find Laurence Harvey attractive. In fact, I think the sooner his present vogue passes the better it will be (it really isn't good for the race for women to want to lean on so frail a reed)." —Ellen Fitzpatrick, *Films in Review*, December 1960

Susan Hayward
I Want to Live, 1958
Academy Award winner for Best Actress.

"In the post-trial and pre-execution scenes Miss Hayward's inadequacies are embarrassing to watch." —Marian Aarons, *Films in Review*, December 1958

Bernard Herrmann ————————————————
Obsession, 1976
    Academy Award nomination for Best Score.

"Worse yet is Herrmann's score, which can't consist of more than eight bars of music, as schmaltzy as the worst of Max Steiner or Victor Young, and becoming louder and nastier with every one of its thousand repetitions.... I don't know what Herrmann died of, but I wouldn't rule out shame as a possibility." —John Simon, *New York*, August 16, 1976

Taxi Driver, 1976
    Academy Award nomination for Best Score and winner of
    the British Academy of Film and Televisions Arts award for
    Best Score.

"...music that is elephantine in its banality and its underlining..." —Stanley Kauffmann, *New Republic*, March 6, 1976

"Matching the cheesily posturing photography is an ungainly and bombastic score by Bernard Herrmann." —John Simon, *New York*, February 23, 1976

Barbara Hershey ————————————————
The Stunt Man, 1980

"She was an attractive adolescent in *Last Summer* 10 years ago; she has grown into an insipid woman." —Stanley Kauffmann, *New Republic*, November 8, 1980

Charlton Heston
The Ten Commandments, 1956

"Charlton Heston, who plays Moses, has a fine hatchet face on which a beard looks well, and nothing else."
—Henrietta Lehman, *Films in Review,* November 1956

Ben-Hur, 1959
  Academy Award winner for Best Actor.

"Heston throws all his punches in the first ten minutes (three grimaces and two intonations) so that he has nothing left four hours later when he has to react to the Crucifixion. (He does make it clear, I must admit, that he disapproves.)." —Dwight Macdonald, *Esquire,* March 1960

Judd Hirsch
King of the Gypsies, 1978

"...perhaps the homeliest actor in Hollywood..."
—Robert Asahina, *New Leader,* January 15, 1979

Alfred Hitchcock
The Birds, 1963

"The only point of interest about *The Birds* is that it's by Alfred Hitchcock, who once had a deserved reputation as a master technician. If the director's name had been, say, Albert Hotchkiss, I should have noted 'tedious and amateurish...perhaps the most spectacularly untalented newcomer since Allen Baron,' and let it go at that...."
—Dwight Macdonald, *Esquire,* November 1963

"Hitchcock's direction has never been so tired, so devoid even of attempts at sardonic realism." —Stanley Kauffmann, *New Republic*, April 13, 1963

Dustin Hoffman
Rain Man, 1988
Academy Award winner for Best Actor.

"He certainly gets points for weirdness, but watching Hoffman bleat and stare into the void and gesture like R2D2, you might wish his stunt had come to more." —David Edelstein, *New York Post*, December 16, 1988

Dennis Hopper
Blue Velvet, 1986

"King of the wackos...Dennis Hopper finally goes as berserk on screen as his reputation indicates offscreen. He holds the record in this one for saying the most F-words in movie history." —Rex Reed, *New York Post*, September 19, 1986

"...comes on like one of Heinrich Himmler's Oberstrumbannfuehrers in country-western drag; and the main technical problem with the scene must have been to keep his droplets of saliva off the lens of the camera..." —Stephen Hunter, *Baltimore Sun*, October 3, 1986

Walter Huston
Rain, 1932

"As the fanatic Davidson, Walter Huston is less the fanatic than the dull bore. As he stalked through his

tense scenes with all the animation of a hoe handle, the
audience reaction instead of tenseness was tit-
ters...." —Cy Caldwell, *New Outlook*, November 1932

Jeremy Irons _____
Dead Ringers, 1988

"...the aptly named Irons puts a metallic pall on the
proceedings...As Bev he's simply a drag—even when the
quiet brother is supposed to be lovable, he seems sinister.
At the outset Bev and Elliot are meant to be like Dr.
Jekyll and Mr. Hyde. The way Irons plays them, they're
simply Dr. Hyde and Mr. Hyde." —Michael Sragow,
San Francisco Examiner, September 23, 1988

"...a severe overdose of Jeremy Irons...this movie is like
a car trip—with him in the backseat of a '54 De Soto—to
Casper, Wyo., as he earnestly explains Why He Became
an Actor...." —Stephen Hunter, *Baltimore Sun*,
September 23, 1988

Sam Jaffe _____
Gunga Din, 1939

"I regret to say that Sam Jaffe was persuaded to play
Gunga Din, a part to which he brings everything, includ-
ing the apparent belief that East is South and that Little
Eva was the natural son of Uncle Tom." —Otis
Ferguson, *New Republic*, February 22, 1939

Tommy Lee Jones
The Fugitive, 1993
    Academy Award and Golden Globe winner for Best
    Supporting Actor.

"A fondly indulged scene stealer in the previous thriller directed by Mr. Davis, *Under Siege,* Mr. Jones is encouraged to dominate *The Fugitive* histrionically as a showboating travesty of the original Gerard." —*Washington Times,* August 6, 1993

Diane Keaton
Annie Hall, 1977
    Academy Award and British Academy of Film and
    Television Arts award for Best Actress.

"And then there is Diane Keaton's scandalous performance.... It is not so much an actress playing a role as a soul in torment crying out for urgent therapy—in bad taste to watch and an indecency to display.... Miss Keaton is allowed to top her acting by singing two songs, which she does even less endurably; to compensate for her lack of vocal endowment, she goes in for even heavier mugging—it might as well be Central Park after dark." —John Simon, *New York,* May 2, 1977

Stanley Kramer
It's a Mad, Mad, Mad, Mad World, 1963

"Kramer's sense of comedy is even more ponderous than his sense of serious drama. He is like the bull in the china shop: his 'comic' touch is like a steady, annoying rap on the head with a hammer; he totally misuses his actors,

giving us their worst, not their best; despite his re-
searches, he has remained for all intents a cinematic
illiterate." —Paul Nelson, *Film Quarterly*, Spring 1964

Stanley Kubrick

Dr. Strangelove, 1963
Academy Award nomination for Best Director.

"And if you have been under any illusion about Kubrick's
competence as a director, look at the absurd performance he allowed George C. Scott to give." —Henry
Hart, *Films in Review*, February 1964

A Clockwork Orange, 1971
Academy Award nomination for Best Screenplay.

"...[Kubrick's] script is adolescent maundering, and
sinks to the depths of buck-chasing (sex scribblings on
walls; total nudity; sight-gags for perverts)." —H.H.,
Films in Review, January 1972

Burt Lancaster

The Sweet Smell of Success, 1957

"...fantastically unbelievable..." —E.F., *Films in
Review*, August/September 1957

David Lean

Dr. Zhivago, 1965

"Imperceptibly, David Lean has evolved into the middlebrow's answer to the late Cecil B. De Mille."
—Andrew Sarris, *Village Voice*, December 30, 1965

John Lithgow
The Adventures of Buckaroo Banzai, 1984

"John Lithgow (who was good in *Terms of Endearment*) plays a homicidal villain possessed by an alien and he does it just like anybody else would on the first day of acting class. He screams and mugs and rolls his eyes." —Michael Healy, *Denver Post,* August 10, 1984

George Lucas
The Empire Strikes Back, 1980

"Lucas should make love, not star wars, to his wife, his dog, his very own television set, and stop contributing to the sappiness of nations." —John Simon, *National Review,* June 13, 1980

David Lynch
Blue Velvet, 1986
    Academy Award nomination for Best Director.

Isabella Rossellini and Kyle MacLachlan in a tense moment in David Lynch's *Blue Velvet*

"He is such an inept director that although I believe he directed such trash wallows as *Eraserhead* and *Dune*, I no longer believe he could have possibly helmed a great film like *The Elephant Man*. Surely Mel Brooks, who produced that one, must have rolled up his sleeves and taken over." —Rex Reed, *New York Post*, September 19, 1986

Shirley MacLaine
Terms of Endearment, 1983
   Academy Award winner for Best Actress.

"MacLaine, saddled with the year's most unflattering wardrobe and hairstyles, appears to be in training to become Hollywood's next Ruth Gordon. Her Aurora is a walking case of premature senility." —Glenn Lovell, *San Jose Mercury*, November 25, 1983

Groucho Marx
Duck Soup, 1933

"Groucho's gags grow staler, and his puns flatter, in every picture. Yet he has more to do in each new opus; his jabber disastrously slows the pace." —Meyer Levin, *Esquire*, February 1934

Giulietta Masina
La Strada, 1956

"As for Giulietta Masina (Fellini's wife), who played the feeble-minded girl, the less said about her the better." —Diana Willing, *Films in Review*, August/September 1956

The Nights of Cabiria, 1957

"...endows the title role with a feeble-minded insou-
ciance which constitutes her acting style. The talk about
Masina's prostitute being equivalent to Chaplin's little
tramp was started by Italian press agents." —L.C.,
Films in Review, December 1957

James Mason
Lolita, 1962

"He never was a very resourceful actor and the best he
can come up with in the emergency is a perspiring
sheepishness punctuated by tantrums and tears. It is
impossible to describe how wearing this becomes."
—Robert Hatch, *Nation,* June 23, 1962

Walter Matthau
Cactus Flower, 1969

"...a modestly pleasant but vastly overrated actor who
looks and acts like Smokey the Bear sleeping through a
four-alarm fire...Walter Matthau continues to draw a
top salary by walking through his roles as though in an
advanced state of hypnosis." —Rex Reed, *Holiday,*
November 1969

Melinia Mercouri
Never on Sunday, 1959
   Academy Award nomination for Best Actress

"Mercouri is a tall, masculine woman who substitutes
flamboyance for acting ability." —Adelaide
Comerford, *Films in Review,* November 1960

Liza Minnelli _____

Cabaret, 1972
> Academy Award, British Academy of Film and Television
> Arts award, Golden Globe winner for Best Actress.

"The film's irredeemable disaster is its Sally Bowles: changing her into an American was bad enough; into Liza Minnelli, catastrophe....Plain, ludicrously rather than pathetically plain is what Miss Minnelli is. That turnipy nose overhanging a forward-gaping mouth and hastily retreating chin, that bulbous cranium with eyes as big (and as inexpressive) as saucers." —John Simon, *New Leader,* March 20, 1972

Lucky Lady, 1975

"As for Miss Minnelli, she is herself a perfect *ménage à trois* in which lack of talent, lack of looks, and lack of a speaking voice cohabit blissfully. Donen sensibly concentrates on her best feature, her legs, but he unfortunately can't wrap them around her face." —John Simon, from his collection *Reverse Angle,* 1982

New York, New York, 1977

"The big difference between Garland and Minnelli is that Garland, though less than comely, was not (until near the end) grotesque and goony; that Garland, even if overacting, did so in her own style at least; and that, though one sometimes refused to cry with Garland, one can never help giggling at Minnelli." —John Simon, *New York*, July 11, 1977

Robert Mitchum

Out of the Past, 1947

"In love scenes his curious languor, which suggests Bing Crosby supersaturated with barbiturates, becomes a brand of sexual complacency that is not endearing." —*Time*, December 15, 1947

Marilyn Monroe

Gentlemen Prefer Blondes, 1953

"Hawks has Marilyn honey and husky her voice, droop her eyelids, protrude her lips, and almost murmur 'come have me' too often. A girl can't keep doing that too long. Even the boys in the back row will stop being affected and begin to watch the technique." —James R. Teple, *Films in Review*, August/September 1953

Bus Stop, 1956

"There has been much publicity recently about Miss Monroe's efforts to become an actress. Only her most faithful admirers will think her performance in *Bus Stop* a step ahead....Maybe Laurence Olivier can help Miss Monroe to become an actress. Joshua Logan and the Actors Studio certainly can't." —Eloise Wood, *Films in Review*, October 1956

Tony Curtis, Jack Lemmon, and Marilyn Monroe in
Some Like It Hot

Some Like It Hot, 1959

"To these sight and situational gags Wilder has also added a plump Marilyn Monroe. I regret to report she is not too much of an addition."   —Ellen Fitzpatrick, *Films in Review*, April 1959

Zero Mostel _____
The Producers, 1968

"Zero Mostel rolls his eyes on the screen as if he were running a bowling alley in his skull."   —Andrew Sarris, *Village Voice*, March 28, 1968

Anthony Newley ———————————————

*Can Hieronymus Merkin Ever Forget Mercy Humppe
and Find True Happiness?*, 1969

"I'm not sure he'll ever work again, and quite frankly, I'm
not sure he deserves to.... The sight of Anthony Newley
naked is enough to make you turn the other way, just
praying you'll turn into a pillar of salt."   —Rex Reed,
Women's Wear Daily, March 21, 1969

Paul Newman ———————————————

The Left-Handed Gun, 1958

"Poor Mr. Newman seems to be auditioning alternately
for the Moscow Art Players and the Grand Old Opry, as
he ambles about, brooding, grinning, or mumbling
endlessly."   —Howard Thompson, *New York Times*, May
8, 1958

Sweet Bird of Youth, 1962

"As for Paul Newman (Chance), well, something will have
to be done about Mr. Newman....He is simply not an
actor and possibly not even alive; seems to be carved
from wood, his movements stiff and jerky as a mar-
ionette, his one expression an agonized grimace as of
wood trying to smile."   —Dwight Macdonald, *Esquire*,
June 1962

Hud, 1963
    Academy Award nomination for Best Actor.

"His woodenly handsome face is still as much his problem as his fortune; I don't know how he can get action
into it, but mouthing his lines is not the way."   —Dwight
Macdonald, *Esquire*, September 1963

The Verdict, 1982
   Academy Award nomination for Best Actor.

"Trying to out-Brando Brando, Newman...makes the character so forlornly hangdog that you wonder how he evaded the dogcatcher, and practically turns his collar inside out so you can marvel at the quantities of ingrained sweat." —John Simon, *National Review,* February 4, 1983

Jack Nicholson
Terms of Endearment, 1983
   Academy Award winner for Best Supporting Actor.

"Nicholson's ex-astronaut is supposed to be a womanizing slob. I realize this. If only the actor didn't fit the roll so completely. It's depressing seeing what an overweight, balding wreck Nicholson has become." —Glenn Lovell, *San Jose Mercury,* November 25, 1983

Peter O'Toole
Lawrence of Arabia, 1963
   Academy Award nomination for Best Actor.

"O'Toole's tormented hermaphrodite (his cerebral tensions conveyed by such a fierce working of cheek musculature it's as if his nerves were on fire) would have had a hard time directing a revolt of disaffected palace eunuchs—let alone a military campaign." —Roger Sandall, *Film Quarterly,* Spring 1963

Gregory Peck
The Omen, 1976

"As for Peck, he worries and suffers as nobly as only a piece of granite can." —John Simon, *New York*, July 12, 1976

MacArthur, 1977

"To tell his years, in fact, you would have to saw him in two and count the rings.... The actor tries to be granite but never gets beyond walnut.... Maybe MacArthur really was like this; if so, he, too, could have been converted very nicely into a coffee table." —John Simon, *New York*, July 11, 1977

Sam Peckinpah
The Wild Bunch, 1969

Ben Johnson, Warren Oates, William Holden, and Ernest Borgnine in Sam Peckinpah's bloody *Wild Bunch*

"There was once hope that Sam Peckinpah might develop into a capable director, but *The Wild Bunch* leads me to the sorry conviction he understands too little of the contemporary scene and has decided, in desperation, to imitate the socio and psycho pathologies with which such anti-life directors as Luis Buñuel and Arthur Penn fill their so-called films." —Arthur B. Clark, *Films in Review*, August/September 1969

Arthur Penn
Bonnie and Clyde, 1967

"Who directed? Arthur Penn, whose artistic integrity is about on the level of Beatty's acting ability—i.e., close to zero." —*Films in Review*, October 1967

Christopher Plummer
The Sound of Music, 1965

"...a former actor who has become a Hollywood leading man..." —Dwight Macdonald, *Esquire*, August 1966

Rob Reiner
When Harry Met Sally, 1989

"Rob Reiner may be a supremely unimaginative, derivative director, but he sure knows who to steal from...." —Bob Strauss, *Los Angeles Daily News*, July 14, 1989

Mickey Rooney
Words and Music, 1948

"Mickey Rooney should never be permitted to play anyone but himself; when he attempts characterization the result is a kind of involuntary libel." —Robert Hatch, *New Republic*, December 27, 1948

Isabella Rossellini
Blue Velvet, 1986

"As for the lovely but misguided Isabella Rossellini, all I can say is that her mother, Ingrid Bergman, must be turning in her grave. If she had lived to see her daughter wobbling naked across somebody's front lawn covered with teeth bites and cigarette burns, she would have probably made a citizen's arrest..." —Rex Reed, *New York Post*, September 19, 1986

Gena Rowlands
A Woman Under the Influence, 1974
  Academy Award nomination for Best Actress. Golden Globe winner for Best Actress.

"Gena Rowlands lets it all hang out ubiquitously and continually; if feelings were laundry, she'd be the city of Naples."—John Simon, *Esquire*, April 1975

"You seem to see her merely mimicking what she has observed through one-way windows in mental hospitals." —Stanley Kauffmann, *New Republic*, December 28, 1974

Rosalind Russell
*Oh Dad, Poor Dad, Mama's Hung You in the Closet and I'm
Feeling So Sad,* 1966

"She used to be funny, but she seems determined lately
to destroy herself and her career by playing every role
she touches like a cross between Auntie Mame and the
Bride of Frankenstein." —Rex Reed, from his collection *Big Screen, Little Screen,* 1971

Susan Sarandon
Atlantic City, 1981
   Academy Award nomination for Best Actress.

"...she charmlessly tries to act avid, lost, and
dumb..." —David Denby, *New York,* April 6, 1981

Paul Schrader
American Gigolo, 1980

"Schrader is that sinister figure Hollywood turns out
intermittently: the hack with a dangerous bit of learn-
ing." —John Simon, *National Review,* April 4, 1980

Martin Scorsese
The Last Waltz, 1978

"What this film demonstrates irrefutably is the ineptness
of Martin Scorsese as a director." —John Simon,
National Review, July 21, 1978

New York, New York, 1977

"The person who comes off least well here is Martin
Scorsese, whose directorial vision seems to be no greater

than that of a man driving through a downpour without turning on his windshield wipers." —John Simon, *New York*, July 11, 1977

Raging Bull, 1980

"He's got moviemaking and the Church mixed up together; he's trying to be the saint of cinema." —Pauline Kael, *New Yorker*, December 8, 1980

Cybill Shepherd
Taxi Driver, 1975

"Cybill Shepherd is pleasant as the blonde (although Scorsese reveals her well-kept secret—her unfortunate legs)." —Stanley Kauffmann, *New Republic*, March 6, 1976

"...it is saddled with Miss Shepherd, whose presence is not even a tribute to Scorsese's healthy appetites: having gained weight, most noticeably in the face, she looks like Mussolini in drag." —John Simon, *New York*, February 23, 1976

James Spader
sex, lies, and videotape, 1989
    Cannes Film Festival prize winner for Best Actor.

"Spader's best-actor prize at Cannes will surely endure as one of the enigmas of the age. Was the jury belatedly honoring his nonsluggish, nonmawkish work in movies like *Pretty in Pink*, *Mannequin*, and *Less Than Zero?*" —Gary Arnold, *The Washington Times*, August 11, 1989

"As for Spader's acting prize, one can only presume the Cannes jury was applauding his casting against type—

usually *he* plays the deceitful greasy yuppie part."
—Edmond Grant, *Films in Review*, October 1989

Sylvester Stallone _____
Rambo: First Blood Part II, 1985

"I have nothing personal against Sylvester Stallone....
But on the screen, he is to acting what Liberace is to
pumping iron." —Rex Reed, *New York Post*, May 22,
1985

Oliver Stone _____
Born on the Fourth of July, 1989
    Academy Award for Best Director.

"His work is pure sensationalism. Armed with his invas-
ive camera, Stone is less an artist than a dictator."
—David Edelstein, *New York Post*, December 20, 1989

Barbra Streisand _____
What's Up, Doc?, 1972

"Miss Streisand looks like a cross between an aardvark
and an albino rat surmounted by a platinum-coated
horse bun. Her speaking voice seems to have graduated
with top honors from the Brooklyn Conservatory of
Yentaism, and her acting consists entirely of fishily
thrusting out her lips, sounding like a cabbie bellyaching
at breakneck speed, and throwing her weight
around." —John Simon, *New Leader*, April 3, 1972

Up the Sandbox, 1972

"I find Miss Streisand's looks repellent. Perhaps this is
my limitation, but I cannot accept a romantic heroine

who is both knock-kneed and ankleless (maybe one of those things, but not both!), short-waisted and shapeless, scrag-toothed and with a horse face centering on a nose that looks like Brancusi's Rooster cast in liverwurst....Streisand remains arrogantly, exultantly ugly...." —John Simon, *New Leader*, February 5, 1973

The Way We Were, 1973
Academy Award nomination for Best Actress.

"...even when Miss Streisand labors to appear sensitive and vulnerable, she cannot conquer our impression that, were she to collide with a Mack truck, it is the truck that would drop dead. And, as always, I am repelled by her looks....Only very plain women, in their wish-fulfillment fantasies, could accept without flinching the dashing Robert Redford's passion for, and bedroom scenes with, Barbra Streisand...." —John Simon, *Esquire,* January 1974

Funny Lady, 1975

"If Miss Streisand did not exist, she would have to be invented, as I believe, she was. There may be uglier women in the world than she is, but surely none that wears her ugliness—enhanced by monumental arrogance-with more bravura (Italian), panache (French), and chutzpah (Yiddish)....All-even the most utterly graceless—can feel, without need for mental sleight of hand, 'There but for the absentmindedness of God, go I.'" —John Simon, *Esquire,* June 1975

A Star is Born, 1976
Golden Globe winner for Best Actress.

"Oh, for the gift of Rostand's Cyrano to evoke the vastness of that nose alone as it cleaves the giant screen from east to west, bisects it from north to south. It zigzags across our horizon like a bolt of fleshy lightning; it towers like a ziggurat made of meat." —John Simon, *New York*, January 10, 1977

The Main Event, 1979

"Dodging that formidable nose in a clinch might be harder than evading the mightiest upper-cut....Directing Steisand must be like trying to get a rogue elephant to cross a street on the green light." —John Simon, *National Review*, August 3, 1979

Donald Sutherland
1900, 1976

"From a brazen ham like Donald Sutherland, we get a performance so appalling that we wonder whether he was directed with a cattle prod." —John Simon, from his collection *Something to Declare*, 1983

Elizabeth Taylor
Raintree County, 1957
   Academy Award nomination for Best Actress.

"A deranged Southern belle (played with whoops, whimpers, and childbed eye-rolling by Elizabeth Taylor)..." —*Time*, January 6, 1958

Butterfield 8, 1960
   Academy Award winner for Best Actress.

"Only in one scene did the face that launches masculine dreams, unfreeze....La Taylor in *Butterfield 8* was merely a clothes horse which Director Mann undressed as often as possible. So often, in fact, I'm sure Joe Ruttenberg got bored turning his camera on her celebrated bust...." —Ellen Fitzpatrick, *Films in Review*, December 1960

Secret Ceremony, 1969

"She has become a hideous parody of herself—a fat, sloppy, yelling, screeching banshee....Miss Taylor in the nude has come to resemble an enormous boiled turnip...." —Rex Reed, *Holiday*, January 1969

The Only Game in Town, 1970

"Now if Elizabeth Taylor wants to go around looking like a Goodyear blimp pumped full of Chasen's chili instead of butane gas, that is her own business. But neither she nor 20th Century-Fox nor George Stevens nor anyone else should expect anyone who hasn't suffered permanent brain damage to believe for one minute that she could be a dancer in a chorus line!" —Rex Reed, *Holiday*, May 1970

Gene Tierney
Laura, 1944

"Laura, who is head of a famous advertising agency (acted by Gene Tierney with no other qualities than there are in a fashion mannequin on parade)." —Manny Farber, *New Republic*, October 30, 1944

Spencer Tracy _____
Dr. Jekyll and Mr. Hyde, 1941

"Mr. Tracy's portrait of Hyde is not so much evil incarnate as it is the ham rampant." —Theodore Strauss,
New York Times, August 13, 1941

The Old Man and the Sea, 1958
   Academy Award nomination for Best Actor.

"He sulked at the director and hardly bothered to act at
all.... In most roles Tracy plays himself, but usually, out
of deference to the part, he plays himself with a difference. This time he plays himself with indifference." —*Time,* October 27, 1958

John Travolta _____
Grease, 1978

"This leaves John Travolta, as the debonair high-school
gang leader. After seeing him in three movies, I am
convinced that he has exhausted his slender bag of
tricks. Even that smiling, blue-eyed colt face of his, like
that of an anthropomorphized Walt Disney horse, has
become a mere whinnying platitude." —John Simon,
National Review, July 21, 1978

Look Who's Talking, 1989

"...the hip-for-fifteen-minutes star of the 70's..."
—Edmond Grant, *Films in Review,* January/February 1990

John Wayne
The Conqueror, 1956

"…He portrays the great conqueror as a sort of cross between a square-shootin' sheriff and a Mongolian idiot. The idea is good for a couple of snickers, but after that it never Waynes but it bores." —*Time*, April 9, 1956

Peter Weller
The Adventures of Buckaroo Banzai, 1984

"Weller is so bland and blasé that he makes little impression at all in the film. He is the dullest superhero imaginable, and has the kind of face that is so impassive as to be nearly invisible. Weller adds new, negative meaning to the phrase 'dead pan.' He brings no humor to the role, and exhibits little life of any sort. And we have to watch him for almost two hours." —Michael Healy, *Denver Post*, August 10, 1984

Orson Welles
Jane Eyre, 1943

"It is possible to enjoy his performance as dead-pan period parody; I imagine he did. I might have more if I hadn't wanted, instead, to see a good performance." —James Agee, *Nation*, February 12, 1944

The Third Man, 1950

"The hamminess of Welles is no longer a joking matter; this youthful bad habit has become a settled vice that

may make him unemployable and a public charge."
—Robert Hatch, *New Republic*, February 6, 1950

Billy Wilder
Sunset Boulevard, 1950

"...a mean director with telescopic eyes..."   —Manny
Farber, *Nation*, September 23, 1950

Bruce Willis
Die Hard, 1988

"Willis is much better suited to his popular jive-talking
TV persona...than to this big-screen action film, in
which he appears in almost every frame, smirking,
cursing, mugging and overacting." —Doris G.
Worsham, *Oakland Tribune*, July 15, 1988

Debra Winger
Terms of Endearment, 1983
   Academy Award nomination for Best Supporting Actress.

"Winger kills this movie. She hams through almost every
scene. Then, when the comic mood of the film suddenly
shifts to tragedy, she can't project any kind of true
pathos. She just starts bawling." —Carol Olten, *San
Diego Union*, November 23, 1983

Natalie Wood
West Side Story, 1961

"Maria, the sweet virgin fresh from Puerto Rico, is the
most machine-tooled of Hollywood ingenues—clever

little Natalie Wood...the newly-constructed love-goddess: so perfectly banal she destroys all thoughts of love." —Pauline Kael, *Film Quarterly*, Summer 1962

William Wyler
Ben-Hur, 1959
Academy Award winner for Best Director.

"The big spectacular moments—the seafight, the Roman triumph, the chariot race—failed because Wyler doesn't know how to handle crowds nor how to get a culminating rhythm by cutting. He tries to make up for this lack by huge sets and thousands of extras, but a Griffith can make a hundred into a crowd while a Wyler can reduce a thousand to a confused cocktail party."
—Dwight Macdonald, *Esquire*, March 1960

5

Trashed Treasures _____

Cult Favorites the Critics Dumped On

The Adventures of Buckaroo Bonzai: Across the 8th Dimension _____
1984

DIRECTOR: W. D. Richter; SCREENPLAY: Earl Mac Rauch;
CAST: Peter Weller, John Lithgow, Ellen Barkin, Jeff
Goldblum.

"...an incoherent mess of a movie, a marketing executive's dream of limitless sales of product rights (Banzai action figures! Banzai comic books! Banzai Home Neurosurgery Kits!) which turned into a nightmare of filmmaking ineptitude...A screenwriter who can't crack a joke; a director who can't direct even the simplest action scenes; a group of actors who chose not to act alive: that is a recipe for a dismal movie."   —Michael Healy, *Denver Post,* August 10, 1984

"The mystique of scientific research and high-tech is fertile ground for satire. But *Buckaroo* sticks its tongue indiscriminately into too many cheeks and degenerates into comic-strip cliches." —Mark Czarnecki, *Macleans*, August 27, 1984

"The filmmakers think they're mocking the routine convolutions of sci-fi; actually, they're drowning in them." —David Edelstein, *Village Voice*, October 16, 1984

Aguirre, Wrath of God
1972

> DIRECTOR: Werner Herzog; SCREENPLAY: Werner Herzog; CAST: Klaus Kinski, Ruy Guerra, Helena Rojo.

"There are long periods of dawdling, after which the film has a brief, spastic forward lurch, only to sink back again into lethargy....The film becomes just the slow picking off of the explorers by here an arrow, there a poison dart, yonder a spear—call it *Ten Little Non-Indians*."—John Simon, *New York*, April 18, 1977

Altered States
1980

> DIRECTOR: Ken Russell; SCREENPLAY: Paddy Chayevsky (using the name Sidney Aaron); CAST: William Hurt, Blair Brown, Bob Balaban.

"What starts out as a jargon-ridden but fascinating story...winds up a sort of 'Dr. Jessup and Mr. Hyde Go to Harvard Medical School.'...Instead of science fiction, we're given endless LSD-oriented trips and a lapse into the staler stuff of horror movies. Big news is that a primal scream can reduce a boiler-room to a shambles." —Judith Crist, *Saturday Review*, February 1981

The American Friend _____
1977

> DIRECTOR: Wim Wenders; SCREENPLAY: Wim Wenders, Fritz
> Muller-Scherz, from the novel *Ripley's Game*, by Patricia
> Highsmith; CAST: Dennis Hopper, Bruno Ganz, Nicholas
> Ray, Samuel Fuller.

"Where, I asked myself as I watched this initially good
picture pound itself to pieces by keeping on and on, was
a producer?...I have rarely been more disgusted by
exceptional photography and editing, used so ego-
centrically." —Stanley Kauffmann, *New Republic,*
October 1, 1977

"...a masterpiece for people who think a movie can't be
worthwhile unless it makes you suffer...Wenders is not
only turgid, he's exhibitionistically turgid." —Pauline
Kael, *New Yorker,* October 17, 1977

Badlands _____
1974

> DIRECTOR: Terrence Malick; SCREENPLAY: Terrence Malick;
> CAST: Martin Sheen, Sissy Spacek, Warren Oates, Ramon
> Bieri.

"Empty, alienating art movies are no longer the novelty
they once were, but *Badlands* represents an insufferable
new synthesis of the form, a *reductio ad absurdum* of the
worst tendencies, both social and cinematic, in *If...,*
Zabriskie Point, A Clockwork Orange, and similar heart-
warmers....In other words, *Badlands* is bad news."
—Gary Arnold, *Washington Post,* May 28, 1974

Barbarella
1968

> DIRECTOR: Roger Vadim; SCREENPLAY: Terry Southern, from the book by Jean-Claude Forest; CAST: Jane Fonda, John Phillip Law, Anita Pallenberg, Milo O'Shea, David Hemmings, Marcel Marceau.

"...the movie, written by Terry Southern and seven other writers and based upon a comic strip, rapidly becomes a special kind of mess...It is a humorist-advertiser's kind of experiment: Let's stab this through the midriff and see if anyone salutes it." —Renata Adler, *New York Times,* October 12, 1968

"...the Dino De Laurentiis production is flawed with a cast that is not particularly adept at comedy, a flat script, and direction of Roger Vadim, which can't get this beached whale afloat..." —*Variety,* October 9, 1968

"Glossy science-fiction trash, which appears to be *2001: A Space Odyssey* seen through the eyes of Helen Gurley Brown and photographed by *Vogue,* and which never makes use of its opportunities, which is okay with me since its opportunities are probably appreciated best by Harvard boys who sit around the *Crimson* office reading *The Story of O* aloud to each other." —Rex Reed, *Holiday,* January 1969

Bedazzled
1967

> DIRECTOR: Stanley Donen; SCREENPLAY: Peter Cook; CAST: Peter Cook, Dudley Moore, Michael Bates, Raquel Welch.

"...pretentiously metaphorical picture...it becomes awfully precious and monotonous and eventually it fags out in sheer bad taste..." —Bosley Crowther, *New York Times,* December 11, 1967

Blood Simple
1984

> DIRECTOR: Joel Coen; SCREENPLAY: Joel and Ethan Coen; CAST: John Getz, Frances McDormand, Dan Hedaya, M. Emmet Walsh.

"The press has widely celebrated *Blood Simple* as a historically important debut and has, in anticipation, been defending it against censure for its gore. The real argument against it is that it's not very good of its kind...in a twelvemonth that saw the debuts of Eagle Pennell (*Last Night at the Alamo*) and Jim Jarmusch (*Stranger Than Paradise*), the Coen brothers seem only smart-ass. No, smart half-ass." —Stanley Kauffmann, *New Republic,* February 25, 1985

A Boy and His Dog
1976

> DIRECTOR: L. Q. Jones; SCREENPLAY: L. Q. Jones, based on a novella by Harlan Ellison; CAST: Don Johnson, Susanne Benton, Jason Robards Jr.

"It manages to be derivative, preposterous, and mildly revolting until the very end, at which point it becomes original, preposterous, and rather more revolting." —John Simon, *New York,* June 21, 1976

"All told, this is the biggest movie disaster in ages." —David Sterritt, *Christian Science Monitor,* June 28, 1976

Breathless (*A Bout de souffle*) ———————————
1960

DIRECTOR: Jean-Luc Godard; SCREENPLAY: Jean-Luc Godard,
from a story by François Truffaut; CAST: Jean-Paul
Belmondo, Jean Seberg, Daniel Boulanger.

"I can quite see that François Truffaut and Jean-Luc
Godard...want to let us know that there is something
wrong with the youth of France. I believe it to be true
and I would like to understand, but coma is a state of
suspension, not a form of communication. And is it
really that easy to steal cars in Paris?" —Robert Hatch,
Nation, March 11, 1961

Brewster McCloud ———————————————
1970

DIRECTOR: Robert Altman; SCREENPLAY: Doran William
Cannon; CAST: Bud Cort, Sally Kellerman, Michael Murphy,
William Windom, Shelley Duvall, René Auberjonois, Stacy
Keach, Margaret Hamilton.

"...the worst movie of a still-young year—possibly one of
the worst movies ever made...*Brewster McCloud* is execr-
able gibberish, out of the minds of kids raised on comic
books...strictly for birdbrains." —Rex Reed, *Holiday,*
August 1969

The Brood ——————————————————————
1979

DIRECTOR: David Cronenberg; SCREENPLAY: David
Cronenberg; CAST: Oliver Reed, Samantha Eggar, Art
Hindle.

"The decline of Samantha Eggar's career is enough to
make a grown man weep. Here is an actress who could

have been one of the most illustrous of our era and she has frittered away her time in trash. If she wants to do horror, why isn't she holding out for Lady Macbeth. One can only conclude she will do anything for money. *The Brood* is a new low for Miss Eggar. What a dreadful picture!" —Scott Cain, *Atlanta Journal,* July 27, 1979

La Cage aux Folles
1978

> DIRECTOR: Edouard Molinaro; SCREENPLAY: Francis Veber, Edouard Molinaro, Marcello Danon, Jean Poiret; CAST: Ugo Tognazzi, Michel Serrault, Michel Galabru.

"There might well be a real movie here, but it is not the one directed by Edouard Molinaro....Mr. Serrault, who won the equivalent to our Oscar for his performance...minces more grossly than ever did Billy De Wolfe, and he lunges at pathos like someone playing right guard for the Rams." —Vincent Canby, *New York Times,* May 13, 1979

Crimes of Passion
1984

> DIRECTOR: Ken Russell; SCREENPLAY: Barry Sandler; CAST: Kathleen Turner, Anthony Perkins, John Laughlin, Annie Potts.

"...a hysterically overheated stew of sex and murder; one to walk away from." —Leslie Halliwell, *Halliwell's Film Guide,* 1994

"...the evocative Kathleen Turner thuds into a wall of inanity in this dismally written, Ken Russell-directed serio-comic examination of sexual morality among American savages..." —*Variety*, September 19, 1984

Cutter's Way
1981, Original Title: *Cutter and Bone*

DIRECTOR: Ivan Passer; SCREENPLAY: Jeffrey Alan Fiskin; CAST: Jeff Bridges, John Heard, Lisa Eichhorn.

"It's smoothly enough made, but it's repellent: and what repels, strange though it may sound about a director in his late 40s, is its juvenility." —Stanley Kauffmann, *New Republic*, August 15, 1981

"It's the sort of picture that never wants to concede what it's about. It is, however, enchanted by the sound of its own dialogue, which is vivid without being informative or even amusing on any level." —Vincent Canby, *New York Times*, March 20, 1981

Diva
1982

DIRECTOR: Jean-Jacques Beineix; SCREENPLAY: Jean-Jacques Beineix, Jean Van Hamme; CAST: Frederic Andrei, Roland Bertin, Richard Bohringer, Wilhelmina Wiggins Fernandez.

"*Diva* is an empty though frightfully chic-looking film from France. Though it means to be a romantic suspense-thriller, it has the self-consciously enigmatic manner of a high-fashion photograph....*Diva* is an anthology of affectations." —Vincent Canby, *New York Times*, April 16, 1982

Dennis Hopper, Peter Fonda, and Jack Nicholson on the road in *Easy Rider*

Easy Rider
1969

DIRECTOR: Dennis Hopper; SCREENPLAY: Peter Fonda, Dennis Hopper, Terry Southern; CAST: Peter Fonda, Dennis Hopper, Jack Nicholson.

Academy Award nominations for Best Story, Screenplay, Best Supporting Actor (Jack Nicholson).

"Hopper, Fonda and their friends went out into America looking for a movie and found instead a small, pious statement (upper case) about our society (upper case), which is sick (upper case). It's pretty but lower case cinema." —Vincent Canby, *New York Times*, July 15, 1969

"There's been a lot of ballyhoo about *Easy Rider*.... It is largely unwarranted.... Mr. Fonda and Mr. Hopper seem to sleepwalk through their parts until the final melodramatic blam. The script, written by them with Terry Southern, is what Cool Hand Luke called a 'failure to communicate.' It seems an endless string of by now trite hipisms. *Easy Rider* is aimed at a young audience—and it is precisely that audience which may be conned by the colorful wrapping on a rather nasty package." — Louise Sweeney, *Christian Science Monitor*, September 29, 1969

Emmanuelle
1974

DIRECTOR: Just Jaeckin; SCREENPLAY: Jean-Louis Richard; CAST: Sylvia Kristel, Marika Green, Alain Cuny.

"Only the French could make such a monumentally boring film about that interesting concern, sex." —John Coleman, *New Statesman*, October 11, 1974

"Anyone who falls for this come-on deserves the movie. *Emmanuelle* could not cause a tingle in the Achilles tendon of a celibate scoutmaster.... Without knowledge of *Deep Throat*, *Emmanuelle* might seem like pretty hot stuff. This gives the film rather too much credit, however. *Emmanuelle* would have to go up against something like *The Greatest Story Ever Told* before it could begin to look titillating." —Jay Cocks, *Time*, January 6, 1975

Eraserhead
1976

DIRECTOR: David Lynch; SCREENPLAY: David Lynch; CAST:
Jack Nance, Charlotte Stewart, Jeanne Bates, Allen Josephs.

"Lynch keeps throwing in graphic close-ups of the
piteous creature, and pulls out all gory stops in the
unwatchable climax. Filmex promo is literally correct
when it calls this 'one of the most repugnant scenes in
film history.'...The mind boggles to learn that Lynch
labored on this pic for five years. Many film students
aspire to be the next Orson Welles or Stanley Kubrick,
but Lynch seems bent on emulating Herschell Gordon
Lewis, the king of low-budget gore." —*Variety*, March
23, 1977

"...a murkily pretentious shocker...aside from the appearance of the tiny monster, it is not a particularly
horrifying film, merely interminable. It runs for close to
two hours, but because of its excruciatingly slow pace
and the underlighting of all its scenes, it seems to be at
least twice that long." —Tom Buckley, *New York Times*,
October 17, 1980

The Fly
1958

DIRECTOR: Kurt Neumann; SCREENPLAY: James Clavell; CAST:
David Hedison, Patricia Owens, Herbert Marshall, Vincent
Price.

"The horror element is somewhat let down by the
banality of the dialogue, but then it is difficult to rise to
the occasion when in conversation with a husband who
drinks milk laced with rum through his antennae, or
whatever it is." —*London Times*, August 4, 1958

Freaks ────────────────────────────
1932

DIRECTOR: Tod Browning; SCREENPLAY: Willis Goldbeck, Leon Gordon; CAST: Wallace Ford, Olga Baclanova, Leila Hyams.

"It is gruesome and uncanny rather than tense, which is where the yarn went off the track. Factors relied upon for effect fail to register properly. The result is a story which does not thrill and at the same time does not please....The real trouble with *Freaks* is it fails to get under the skin." —*Variety*, July 12, 1932

The Gods Must Be Crazy ──────────────
1980

DIRECTOR: Jamie Uys; SCREENPLAY: Jamie Uys; CAST: N!xau, Marius Weyers, Sandra Prinsloo.

"With the sort of crude dubbing not usually encountered outside of 42d Street grindhouses, *Gods* errs in way overdoing hackneyed comedy devices....Pic's success in France (where Jerry Lewis and the late Louis de Funes are so popular) is not surprising nor is its conquering of unsophisticated markets, but the U.S. is another story....Uys's sledgehammer direction is technically inadequate, with crude editing and other gimmickry." —*Variety*, July 4, 1984

Greetings ──────────────────────────
1968

DIRECTOR: Brian De Palma; SCREENPLAY: Charles Hirsch, Brian De Palma; CAST: Jonathan Warden, Robert De Niro, Gerrit Graham, Megan McCormick.

"*Greetings,* a free-wheeling exercise put together by a group of chaps in their 20s, is way off target.... Most of it is strained and unfunny, with some generous nudity for nudity's sake and a hip sprinkling of four-letter words.... Next time they might try for something that matters instead of the tired, tawdry and tattered."
—Howard Thompson, *New York Times,* December 16, 1968

Gun Crazy
1950

> DIRECTOR: Joseph H. Lewis; SCREENPLAY: MacKinlay Kantor, Dalton Trumbo; CAST: Peggy Cummins, John Dall, Barry Kroeger, Annabel Shaw.

"The main drawbacks are the stars themselves, who look more like fugitives from a 4-H Club than from the law.... At the risk of being drilled between the eyes by one of these sureshots, we must say that it takes more than crime and the King Brothers to make sows' ears out of silk purses."   —Howard Thompson, *New York Times,* August 25, 1950

Harold and Maude
1971

> DIRECTOR: Hal Ashby; SCREENPLAY: Colin Higgins; CAST: Bud Cort, Ruth Gordon, Vivian Pickles, Cyril Cusack.

"Harold and Maude has all the fun and gaiety of a burning orphanage.... One thing that can be said about Ashby—he began the film in a gross and macabre manner, and never once deviates from the concept. That's style for you." —*Variety*, December 15, 1971

"The moral seems to be that you cannot mix black comedy with dewy sentiment, and when Harold and Maude contemplate marriage after apparently spending the night together, the mixture begins to taste distinctly brackish." —Tom Milne, *London Times*, April 28, 1972

House of Wax
1953

DIRECTOR: Andre de Toth; SCREENPLAY: Crane Wilbur; CAST: Vincent Price, Carolyn Jones, Paul Picerni.

"Its capacity to scare anyone but the hopelessly credulous is open to serious question, and its capacity to interest without scaring is even more negligible. Consequently, for *adults* its bag of technical tricks remains just that." —Moira Walsh, *America*, May 23, 1953

In the Realm of the Senses (*Ai No Corrida*)
1976

DIRECTOR: Nagisa Oshima; SCREENPLAY: Nagisa Oshima; CAST: Tatsuya Fuji, Eiko Matsuda, Aoi Nakajima, Meika Seri.

"The fancy decor, the geisha trimmings, the cinematic attitudinizing don't elevate it beyond a demonstration of stamina that finally reaches the pathological....*Realm* is *at best* a sentimentally fallacious film, an Oriental *Elvira Madigan* undressed, exalted for some by its close ups of screwing." —Stanley Kauffmann, *New Republic*, July 2, 1977

It's a Mad, Mad, Mad, Mad World
1964

DIRECTOR: Stanley Kramer; SCREENPLAY: William and Tania Rose; CAST: Spencer Tracy, Jimmy Durante, Milton Berle, Sid Caesar, Ethel Merman, Buddy Hackett, Mickey Rooney, Dick Shawn, Phil Silvers, Terry-Thomas, Jonathan Winters, Edie Adams.

"From beginning to end, *Mad, Mad World* is a real horror film, peopled with grotesques and directed by a blind man.... Kramer has taken a script which he calls 'the funniest ever written'...and methodically turned it into a dull and deadly chase 'comedy.'"   —Paul Nelson, *Film Quarterly*, Spring 1964

It's Alive!
1974

DIRECTOR: Larry Cohen; SCREENPLAY: Larry Cohen; CAST: John Ryan, Sharon Farrell, Andrew Duggan, Guy Stockwell.

"If we consider the course of the American thriller over the past several years; the idea of a movie about a homicidal baby becomes not so much shocking as inevitable. Somebody had to do it sooner or later. Actually, *It's Alive!* was done sooner; it's been lying around Hollywood for at least a year and only this week came crawling to a number of area theaters....primarily the movie, like the baby, goes animalistically for the jugular. It's frightening more for its own cold ruthlessness than for what happens on the screen."   —Tom Shales, *Washington Post*, September 4, 1976

Johnny Guitar
1954

DIRECTOR: Nicholas Ray; SCREENPLAY: Philip Yordan; CAST: Joan Crawford, Mercedes McCambridge, Sterling Hayden.

"It is all hopelessly unconvincing and foolish, but because it is acted with such dedicated earnestness and is, in a sense, a parody of itself, it gives a perverted pleasure, the corpses with which the ground is strewn at the end raising to a crescendo the laughter which dogs this poor unsuspecting film." —Virginia Graham, *Spectator,* June 4, 1954

"Actually the story and impressive cast could have made an interesting outdoor movie; but director Nicholas Ray seemingly refused to take the script or his actors seriously. He just couldn't have planned the theatrical entrances and poses Crawford assumes, the ham manner in which McCambridge shrieks her lines or the indifference of the various men involved." —Philip T. Hartung, *Commonweal,* June 18, 1954

"Most of them are twice as large as life and three times as ridiculous, and the unfortunate males (Sterling Hayden, Scott Brady) are given short shrift by the script." —Moira Walsh, *America,* June 5, 1954

"Actress McCambridge...achieves a believable, blank-mask expression of insanity. The other performers seem bewildered most of the time by the direction of Nicholas Ray...who works with the misguided brilliance of a myopic Pygmalion." —*Time,* June 14, 1954

King of Hearts _____
1966

DIRECTOR: Philippe de Broca; Screenplay; Daniel Boulanger; CAST: Alan Bates, Genevieve Bujold, Jean-Claude Brialy.

"For a truly tiresome anti-war movie, the kind that makes you want to enlist and give Kaiser Bill a crack on the snout, I nominate *King of Hearts,* a smug little bonbon out of France." —Wilfrid Sheed, *Esquire,* July 1967

The Long Goodbye _____
1973

DIRECTOR: Robert Altman; SCREENPLAY: Leigh Brackett, from the novel by Raymond Chandler; CAST: Elliott Gould, Nina Van Pallandt, Sterling Hayden.

"The movie opens with a rasping fanfare, a blast from an old record of "Hooray for Hollywood." It very neatly sets the tone for this travesty of Raymond Chandler's superb novel about honor and friendship, two subjects among a great many that Robert Altman cannot bring himself to take seriously....Any resemblance between Chandler's book and this movie is not only coincidental but probably libelous." —Jay Cocks, *Time,* April 9, 1973

Lost in America _____
1985

DIRECTOR: Albert Brooks; SCREENPLAY: Albert Brooks, Monica Johnson; CAST: Albert Brooks, Julie Hagerty.

"*Lost in America* could serve as a text for how to sabotage a comedy....the script is a mess. It's a series of sketches instead of a movie." —Joseph Gelmis, *Newsday*, February 15, 1985

"Like his earlier pictures, this one runs out of gas after a while; then it just stops." —David Denby, *New York*, February 25, 1985

The Man Who Fell to Earth
1976

> DIRECTOR: Nicolas Roeg; SCREENPLAY: Paul Mayersburg; CAST: David Bowie, Rip Torn, Candy Clark.

"It is sick with *chic*.... It is extremely hard not to say how dire, albeit drastically handsome, this olio is." —John Coleman, *New Statesman*, March 19, 1976

"All in all, it's a witless venture, tritely sardonic and covering its unresolved implications with outer-space photographic swirls and high-frequency squeals." —Robert Hatch, *Nation*, June 19, 1976

"As always in a Roeg film, there is a good deal of sexual intercourse, which gets intercut with something else. Here it is intercut with more intercourse—spatial intercourse, which differs from the terrestrial kind in that it is more boring to watch.... What is most on display, though, is Roeg's third-rate sensibility desperately aspiring to the second-rate." —John Simon, *New York*, June 14, 1976

Marnie
1964

> DIRECTOR: Alfred Hitchcock; SCREENPLAY: Jay Presson Allen; CAST: Sean Connery, Tippi Hedren, Martin Gabel, Diane Baker.

"Alfred Hitchcock's *Marnie* is nothing less than a disaster.... Why Hitchcock should have thought that this textbook case history should be worth making into a movie is puzzling enough. But the real mystery is why his technique is as inept as that of the greenest novice.... Sean Connery is adequate, which in a picture like this is a great achievement." —*Newsweek*, August 3, 1964

"Another of his Psychology I primers, it commits what is, for Hitchcock, the unpardonable sin: it never stops talking.... It might conceivably satisfy an audience that has nothing more stimulating than a commercial to look forward to, but certainly not anyone who remembers Hitchcock in his prime." —Arthur Knight, *Saturday Review*, September 5, 1964

Mommie Dearest
1981

DIRECTOR: Frank Perry; SCREENPLAY: Frank Yablans, Frank Perry, Tracy Hotchner, Robert Getchell; CAST: Faye Dunaway, Diana Scarwid, Steve Forrest.

"Whatever the truth, director Frank Perry's portrait here is sorry indeed.... What finally must be said is that nobody ever lived a life that deserved this." —Variety, September 9, 1981

"Confronted by a movie without narrative tension or human interest, one is finally reduced to watching the paint dry—on Dunaway's face." —Richard Schickel, *Time*, September 21, 1981

"Adapted by an unholy quartet of screenwriters and directed by the insensitive and maladroit Frank Perry,

Mommie Dearest is very straightforwardly a horror movie...For lovers of the outlandish, the inept, the ineffably absurd." —David Denby, *New York,* September 28, 1981

Morgan!
1966

DIRECTOR: Karel Reisz; SCREENPLAY: David Mercer, from his play; CAST: Vanessa Redgrave, David Warner.

"The British import *Morgan!* (the exclamation mark is because the name is constantly being shouted in exasperation) raises an interesting point in the strategy of fiction—to what degree is it feasible to victimize the audience?...*Morgan!* is a very smart film—in the end, it outsmarts itself." —Robert Hatch, *Nation,* April 25, 1966

One-Eyed Jacks
1961

DIRECTOR: Marlon Brando; SCREENPLAY: Guy Trosper, Calder Willingham; CAST: Marlon Brando, Karl Malden, Pina Pellicer.

"Someone gave Marlon Brando enough rope and he hanged himself. I have seen a lot of extravagant praise— or at least a batch of exhilarated excerpts—for *One Eyed Jacks,* but it is really patronizing Mr. Brando to pretend that he is a good director. The film runs (down-hill) for more than two hours; it is lushly beautiful and mushily sentimental, implausible and inconsequential." —Robert Hatch, *Nation,* April 15, 1961

"...not only childish and neurotic but also the lowest point in an acting career which has been steadily more disappointing...*One-Eyed Jacks* is such an egregiously self-indulgent film. The character that Mr. Brando has been playing for some years now has never had such an uncorseted exposition, doubtless because Mr. Brando was here his own director." —Dwight Macdonald, *Esquire*, October 1961

The Parallax View ─────────────────────────
1974

> DIRECTOR: Alan J. Pakula; SCREENPLAY: David Giler, Lorenzo Semple Jr.; CAST: Warren Beatty, Paula Prentiss, William Daniels.

"A complete fraud any way you look at it...The plot of this purported thriller has more holes than Second Avenue." —Philip Nobile, Lee Eisenberg, *National Review,* November 8, 1974

"Though a touch of paranoid fantasizing can energize an entertainment, too much of it is just plain crazy—neither truthful nor useful. And certainly nothing for responsible men to try to make a buck with in the movies." —Richard Schickel, *Time,* July 8, 1974

"I can't recall another movie that seemed to be so far out of creative control." —Malcolm Boyd, *Christian Century*, August 7, 1974

Pee-Wee's Big Adventure ──────────────────
1985

> DIRECTOR: Tim Burton; SCREENPLAY: Phil Hartman, Paul Reubens, Michael Varhol; CAST: Paul Reubens, Elizabeth Daily, Mark Holton.

"Anyone who laughs at *Pee-Wee's Big Adventure* ought to be put through an airport metal detector.... I wanted to leave... after five minutes. I stayed, much to my pain, for all 92. I think I'll go see *I Spit on Your Grave* to try to cheer up." —Gene Siskel, *Chicago Tribune*, August 12, 1985

"His big mystery lies in his strange appeal for adolescents.... Fair warning: this movie could induce terminal boredom in adults and rot the minds of the young." —*Time*, August 26, 1985

"Mr. Herman resembles a miniature Stan Laurel, but only physically. He is a gimmick that doesn't work, from his too-small glen-plaid suit and red bow tie to the self-satisfied smile with which he continually compliments his own petulant humor. The movie has the cartoonish realism of a Muppet movie. However, Mr. Herman is no Kermit the Frog, although he made me feel like Oscar the Grouch." —Julie Salamon, *Wall Street Journal*, August 13, 1985

"...the film was like a nightmare that left an indelible impression of Pee-Wee Herman himself, simpering, mincing, smiling his tight little smile, eternally hopeful. But the action itself remains a total blank. I remember him so well that it blots out all recollection of what he did.... Herman's spasmodic motor response must be the secret of his communication with the large world of teenage uncertitude. An adult can only wonder, unless decently retarded." —Archer Winsten, *New York Post*, August 9, 1985

"I find Herman about as appetizing as warmed-over spinach (a dish which presumably also has its admirers), and was unable to digest even a small portion of the comic's feature-film debut.... *Adventure* strikes me as the most thoroughly excruciating cinematic exercise in idiot comedy since Steve Martin's comparably puerile *The Jerk*....As for me, I hope never to lay eyes on his miserable red bowtie again." —David Baron, *New Orleans Times-Picayune*, August 15, 1985

Petulia
1968

DIRECTOR: Richard Lester; SCREENPLAY: Lawrence B. Marcus; CAST: George C. Scott, Julie Christie, Richard Chamberlain.

"*Petulia* is a dazzlement of props and locations shots, around which the actors ricochet helplessly through a non-romance between a girl who is some kind of nut and an orthopedic surgeon who seems to be going the same route." —*Time*, June 14, 1968

"The action is athletic and lachrymose, the props are kooky, the music is bright, the domestic sets are suitable for the reading of *Playboy*, there is an adequate amount of surgical duress. Given such attractions it is perhaps churlish to pine for the antique virtues of a beginning, a middle, and an end." —Robert Hatch, *Nation*, July 8, 1968

"...it was obvious to all Lester didn't know what he was doing. Neither did the scriptwriter...Just to put the lid on: two musical—so called—aggregations with the repulsive names of *The Grateful Dead* and *Big Brother and the Holding Company* are worked in to this incompetency." —Rachel Weisbrod, *Films in Review*, June/July 1968

Picnic at Hanging Rock ————————————
1975

> DIRECTOR: Peter Weir; SCREENPLAY: Cliff Green; CAST:
> Rachel Roberts, Dominic Guard, Helen Morse.

"What he is pushing as metaphysical profundity is closer
to metaphysical mush." —David Ansen, *Newsweek*,
March 5, 1979

Pretty Baby ————————————
1978

> DIRECTOR: Louis Malle; SCREENPLAY: Polly Platt, Louis Malle;
> CAST: Keith Carradine, Susan Sarandon, Brooke Shields.

"The picture is too rotten to be worth much of a fuss; it's
worth just enough attention to show why it's rotten."
—Stanley Kauffmann, *New Republic*, April 15, 1978

The Producers ————————————
1968

> DIRECTOR: Mel Brooks; SCREENPLAY: Mel Brooks; CAST: Zero
> Mostel, Gene Wilder, Kenneth Mars.

"Director Brooks has given author Brooks, and us,
possibly the worst movie of the year. Even worse, director
Brooks has committed the absolutely unpardonable sin of
making Zero Mostel appear obnoxious." —Dan Bates,
Film Quarterly, Summer 1968

"The star not only indulges himself gluttonously, but the
director seems to be doubled up with laughter at how
funny *he* is being through Mostel; and the film bloats

into sogginess.... The next time Mostel makes a film I hope it won't be with friends." —Stanley Kauffmann, *New Republic*, April 13, 1968

"Readers will have to accept much of what follows on faith—unless they care to check on me by seeing the picture themselves, a course I do not recommend.... What is required is a steadily accelerating rhythm of belly laughs, and in this respect *The Producers* is worse than disappointing, it is frustrating to the point of physical distress. At least, I find two hours of aborted laughter a strain on the system." —Robert Hatch, *Nation*, April 8, 1968

"Except for two or three expert sequences, the direction of Mel Brooks is thoroughly vile and inept. Everyone in the film down to the least extra mugs with an extravagance not seen since the most florid silent days..." —Andrew Sarris, *Village Voice*, March 28, 1968

The Rain People _____
1969

DIRECTOR: Francis Ford Coppola; SCREENPLAY: Francis Ford Coppola; CAST: Shirley Knight, James Caan, Robert Duvall.

"There are films that are made up of surface images, and once you have seen those images nothing is left and the film disappears. That is *The Rain People*." —Jerry De Muth, *Christian Century*, December 31, 1969

Raising Arizona _____
1987

DIRECTOR: Joel Coen; SCREENPLAY: Ethan Coen, Joel Coen; CAST: Nicolas Cage, Holly Hunter, John Goodman, Trey Wilson.

"The astonishing thing about *Raising Arizona* is how it can move so fast, be so loud, and remain so relentlessly boring at the same time....*Raising Arizona is* miraculously adept technically....But all this wizardry is in the service of really cretinous humor and a deeply condescending viewpoint." —Sheila Benson, *Los Angeles Times*, March 20, 1987

"*Raising Arizona* is a clown film. It comes on with an outsize painted funny face all over its plot and technique and performances, insisting from the start that it's hilarious because its face says it is. The result, from the start, is stupefyingly boring." —Stanley Kauffmann, *New Republic*, April 13, 1987

"Mr. Cage and Miss Hunter, who should carry the movie, go at their roles with a tenacity that the film itself never makes adequate use of. They less often prompt spontaneous pleasure than the recognition that they're supposed to be funnier and more endearing than they manage to be. *Raising Arizona* may well be a comedy that's more entertaining to read than to see." —Vincent Canby, *New York Times*, March 11, 1987

Repo Man
1984

> DIRECTOR: Alex Cox; SCREENPLAY: Alex Cox; CAST: Harry Dean Stanton, Emilio Estevez, Tracey Walter.

"The world of automobile repossessors is about as fascinating as a barrel of dead spiders. Somebody at Universal has been mesmerized enough, however, to flush down the drain more money than most of us will ever see in our bank statements, on a piece of trash called *Repo Man*....It stinks from here to Pasadena." —Rex Reed, *New York Post*, July 6, 1984

Reservoir Dogs _____
1992

> DIRECTOR: Quentin Tarantino; SCREENPLAY: Quentin
> Tarantino; CAST: Harvey Keitel, Tim Roth, Michael Madsen,
> Steve Buscemi.

"...the show never ceases to look and sound like a total
crock. And an excessively brutal total crock at
that....Quentin Tarantino shovels on the hyperbole. He
serves the brutality steaming raw, so to speak, but you
won't miss anything nourishing or revelatory if you skip
the entire cannibal's banquet." —Gary Arnold,
Washington Times, October 24, 1992

Return of the Secaucus Seven _____
1981

> DIRECTOR: John Sayles; SCREENPLAY: John Sayles; CAST: Mark
> Arnott, Gordon Clapp, Maggie Cousineau, John Sayles.

"I must confess at the outset my astonishment at the
glowing reviews garnered elsewhere by this piece of
sophomoric claptrap....I can only say that, by demon-
strating that one can make an utterly mediocre film on
$60,000 just as easily as on $6 million, *Secaucus* goes a
long way toward demolishing the well-meaning if essentially quixotic contention that low budgets are the surest
guarantee of artistic (or, better yet, *meaningful*) motion
pictures." —David Baron, *New Orleans Times-Picayune,*
August 25, 1981

The Road Warrior (also known as Mad Max II) ——
1981

DIRECTOR: George Miller; SCREENPLAY: Terry Hayes, George
Miller, Brian Hannant; CAST: Mel Gibson, Bruce Spence,
Vernon Wells, Emil Minty.

"What all true believers will want to know is: has success
spoiled Mad Max? And I'm afraid the answer is a
resounding yes." —Michael Sragow, *Rolling Stone,* June
24, 1982

"The movie is a demolition derby crossed with gladi-
atorial combat. When it finally runs out of corpses, it
stops.... Maybe people who are bored with the complex-
ities of better movies will find the kill-or-be-killed nihilism a turn-on. Everyone else, I think, will just be worn
down by *The Road Warrior*." —David Denby, *New York,*
August 30, 1982

"A mass of post-holocaust desert traffic maimingly directed by Australian George Miller, begetter of its
equally silly and nasty box-office winner and predeces-
sor, *Mad Max...*" —John Coleman, *New Statesman,*
March 5, 1982

The Rocky Horror Picture Show ——————
1975

DIRECTOR: Jim Sharman; SCREENPLAY: Richard O'Brien;
CAST: Tim Curry, Susan Sarandon, Barry Bostwick, Richard
O'Brien, Patricia Quinn, Charles Gray, Little Nell, Meatloaf.

"The camp sensibility of the author-composer, Richard
O'Brien, takes such an insistently knowing but ultimately

Richard O'Brien, Tim Curry, and Patricia Quinn in
The Rocky Horror Picture Show

humorless form that one may need to be clinically
interested in or emotionally committed to his big preoccupation, transvestism, to get in the peculiar spirit of the
show for any length of time....If you aren't mightily
amused at the way Curry comes on...the proceedings
are going to degenerate from the merely weird to the
positively tedious." —Gary Arnold, *Washington Post,*
January 28, 1976

"*The Rocky Horror Picture Show* could be called poor man's
Ken Russell except that would be a question of overesti-
mated wealth. Destitute would be more like it...the very
shallow material falls apart when viewed through director

Sharman's flat camera work. Music by O'Brien is derivative, repetitive, and generally dull. Humor is obvious and played too broadly for the screen." —Richard Dodds, *New Orleans Times-Picayune,* September 29, 1976

Seconds
1966

> DIRECTOR: John Frankenheimer; SCREENPLAY: Lewis John Carlino; CAST: Rock Hudson, Salome Jens, Will Greer, John Randolph.

"John Frankenheimer, the director, and Lewis John Carlino, the screenwriter, have made *Seconds* a film of almost insupportable ugliness, and if they meant it to be what it is they must both be as mad as March hares." —Joseph Morgenstern, *Newsweek,* October 17, 1966

"Frankenheimer starts off his Faustian sci-fi fable so intensely and so unpleasantly that even horror becomes a kind of comedy relief. Besides, the plot...is not much more plausible than the plot of *Damn Yankees,* and *Damn Yankees* had Gwen Verdon." —Andrew Sarris, *Village Voice,* October 13, 1966

Targets
1968

> DIRECTOR: Peter Bogdanovich; SCREENPLAY: Peter Bogdanovich; CAST: Boris Karloff, Tim O'Kelly, James Brown.

"It seems to me a fantastically foolish picture. How intellectually chaotic to make a gun-control parable that is so empty of any sense of the people in it that the only response left to an audience is to recline with a bag of popcorn and lust after a manly score of assassinations." —Penelope Gilliatt, *New Yorker,* September 7, 1968

The Thing
1951

> DIRECTOR: Howard Hawks; SCREENPLAY: Charles Lederer, from the story *Who Goes There,* by J. W. Campbell Jr.; CAST: Robert Cornthwaite, Kenneth Tobey, Margaret Sheridan.

"The New York theatre at which *The Thing* is shown employs a pretty girl in nursing garb to care for overwrought patrons, but I think the management underestimates the capacity of metropolitan audience to withstand the spectacle of a large man swathed in bandages who pushes through breakaway scenery and emits hoarse grunts. This picture won't be really horrible until Abbott and Costello join the cast." —Robert Hatch, *New Republic,* May 21, 1951

"...lacks genuine entertainment values." —*Variety,* April 4, 1951

Two-Lane Blacktop
1971

> DIRECTOR: Monte Hellman; SCREENPLAY: Rudolph Wurlitzer, Will Corry; CAST: James Taylor, Warren Oates, Laurie Bird, Dennis Wilson.

"Although *Two-Lane Blacktop* is supposed to go from Texas to Washington, it never really goes anywhere." —Louise Sweeney, *Christian Science Monitor,* July 9, 1971

"It's difficult to imagine a dimmer reflection of that somewhat amorphous culture being made, even by the sort of medium-hip 'independent' Hollywood hacks responsible for this film. Certainly no embodiments of Youthful America could surpass the unprofessional and uncharismatic natures of James Taylor, Dennis Wilson, and Laurie Bird, whose screen presences are almost laughably vacuous. *Two-Lane Blacktop* tries to be a, you know, Heavy Trip, but it's been conceived by lightweight minds and cast with lightweight personalities." —Gary Arnold, *Washington Post,* July 20, 1971

Up in Smoke
1978

> DIRECTOR: Lou Adler; SCREENPLAY: Cheech Marin, Tommy Chong; CAST: Cheech Marin, Tommy Chong, Stacy Keach, Tom Skerritt.

"Except for its appeal to the less sophisticated members of the 60s–70s hip subculture, this crude and belabored film directed by Lou Adler ought to be a real drug on the market....It's definitely not for impressionable teens or younger kids. Or for sensible adults either." —Malcolm Johnson, *Hartford Courant,* October 3, 1978

"*Up in Smoke*—that's exactly where this Cheech and Chong comedy goes after a reel or two." —Kevin Thomas, *Los Angeles Times,* September 29, 1978

"...one of the most juvenile, poorly written, awkwardly directed pictures I have ever seen...if the pot-smokers of Chicago—to whom this film is pitched—if they make *Up in Smoke* a local hit, then it will have been proven that 'marijuana rots the brain'..." —Gene Siskel, *Chicago Tribune*, September 26, 1978

Walkabout
1971

DIRECTOR: Nicholas Roeg; SCREENPLAY: Edward Bond; CAST: Jenny Agutter, Lucien John, David Gumpilil.

"I found it specious, over-facile and unnecessarily gruesome.... I was stunned, moreover, to discover later that the film is based on a book regarded as the *Swiss Family Robinson* of Australia, for the movie abounds in phallic symbolism and other exotic erotic intimations." —Moira Walsh, *America*, July 24, 1971

"Roeg and his scenarist Edward Bond (*Blow-Up*) aim for the mind and miss wildly. Their preachy, anti-intellectulal Natural Mannerisms are neither convincing nor new." —Stefan Kanfer, *Time*, June 28, 1971

Where the Boys Are
1960

DIRECTOR: Henry Levin; SCREENPLAY: George Wells, based on the novel by Glendon Swarthout; CAST: Dolores Hart, George Hamilton, Yvette Mimieux, Jim Hutton, Barbara Nichols, Paula Prentiss, Connie Francis.

"A little bit shocking and sad...because the sex-hipped behavior it demonstrates is dished up as though it were the funniest and most natural sort of thing for college kids.... It looks and sounds like a chummy dramatization of the Kinsey reports." —Bosley Crowther, *New York Times*, January 20, 1961

Where's Poppa? ————————————————————
1970

> DIRECTOR: Carl Reiner; SCREENPLAY: Robert Klane, from his
> novel; CAST: George Segal, Ruth Gordon, Trish Van Devere.

"Worse than the obscenities provided by Mr. Reiner is the insensitivity to anguishing problems he and his coworkers reveal. But to go any further would be to enter the territory of the pathological." —Hollis Alpert, *Saturday Review,* November 28, 1970

"It was not for nothing that Reiner was the greatest second banana in TV history; it was for next to nothing. His film is but a single joke, and the punch line is the commonplace twelve-letter obscenity." —Stefan Kanfer, *Time,* December 14, 1970

"If you have been waiting to see Ruth Gordon bite George Segal's left buttock, this picture is for you." —Stanley Kauffmann, *New Republic,* December 5, 1970

Zardoz ————————————————————
1973

> DIRECTOR: John Boorman; SCREENPLAY: John Boorman;
> CAST: Sean Connery, Charlotte Rampling, John Alderton.

"…demonstrates how one can make a cheap sci-fi flick look like a cheap sci-fi flick by using mirrors and prisms as substitutes for imagination." —Judith Crist, *New York,* February 11, 1974

6

Appalling!

Movies That Shocked and Outraged the Tender Sensibilities of the Critics

Alien
1979

DIRECTOR: Ridley Scott; SCREENPLAY: Dan O'Bannon; CAST: Sigourney Weaver, Tom Skerritt, John Hurt.

"Occasionally one sees a film that uses the emotional resources of movies with such utter cynicism that one feels sickened by the medium itself. *Alien*...is so 'effective' it has practically turned me off movies altogether.... The movie is terrifying, but not in a way that is remotely enjoyable." —David Denby, *New York,* June 4, 1979

Baby Doll
1956

DIRECTOR: Elia Kazan; SCREENPLAY: Tennessee Williams, from his play; CAST: Karl Malden, Eli Wallach, Carroll Baker, Mildred Dunnock.

Academy Award nominations for Best Screenplay, Cinematography, Actress (Carroll Baker), Supporting Actress (Mildred Dunnock).

"In defending his production and direction of this culturally worthless and socially debasing film, Elia Kazan said he believes it depicts reality....*Baby Doll* is not realism. It is merely a literary trick, whereby the more complicated and degenerate kinds of smut are covered over with pseudo social significance....Whatever power *Baby Doll* may possess derives from no technique other than the technique of exciting audiences to wonder what depravity is coming next." —H. H., *Films in Review,* January 1957

The Big Heat
1953

DIRECTOR: Fritz Lang; SCREENPLAY: Sydney Boehm; CAST: Glenn Ford, Gloria Grahame, Alexander Scourby.

"The present vogue for sadism and violence reaches some kind of apex in *The Big Heat,* a truly gruesome crime thriller....There is, of course, no excuse at all for a film like *The Big Heat.*" —Robert Kass, *Catholic World,* October 1953

The Blob
1958

DIRECTOR: Irwin S. Yeaworth Jr.; SCREENPLAY: Theodore Simonson, Kate Phillips; CAST: Steve McQueen, Aneta Corseaut, Olin Howlin.

"The real horror is that these pictures, with their bestialities, their sadism, their lust for blood, and their primitive level of conception and execution should find their greatest acceptance among the young. It is sad enough as a commentary on our youth, but even more so on the standards of our motion-picture industry." —Arthur Knight, *Saturday Review*, October 18, 1958

Bloody Mama
1969

> DIRECTOR: Roger Corman; SCREENPLAY: Robert Thom; CAST: Shelley Winters, Pat Hingle, Don Stroud, Diane Varsi, Bruce Dern, Clint Kimbrough, Robert De Niro.

"Imitation, as practiced by American International Pictures, is the most shameless form of debasement. *Bloody Mama*, with Shelley Winters as Ma Barker, takes the bare bones of *Bonnie and Clyde* but leaves the beauty and brains behind....I can understand some people relishing this film: would-be gun slingers for whom the country is insufficiently violent, rural and urban victims of an educational system tht enlightens the rich and imprisons the poor....What I can't understand is how critics who are supposed to know a bit more than the commonest man can discuss such a movie as anything but a shrewd commercial exercise." —Joseph Morgenstern, *Newsweek*, May 25, 1970

Blue Velvet
1986

> DIRECTOR: David Lynch; SCREENPLAY: David Lynch; CAST: Kyle MacLachlan, Isabella Rossellini, Dennis Hopper.
>
> Academy Award nomination for Best Director.

"One of the sickest films ever made…In the brain-damaged garbage department, *Blue Velvet* gives pretentiousness new meaning. It should score high with the kind of sickos who like to smell dirty socks and pull the wings off butterflies, but there's nothing here for sane audiences….Bring a barf bag." —Rex Reed, *New York Post*, September 19, 1986

"In *Blue Velvet*, writer-director David Lynch gets ample opportunity to do what he does best: nauseate an audience….Advance reviews have praised it under the mantle of art, but if this is the state of the art, many of us will be proud to join the ranks of the Philistines." —David Lida, *Women's Wear Daily*, September 19, 1986

"What's worse? Slapping somebody around, or standing back and finding the whole thing funny?" —Roger Ebert, from his *Movie Home Companion*, 1993.

"…offensive and dangerously misleading, a sick joke masquerading as an exploration of evil in the world…Maybe *Blue Velvet* is winning accolades because critics are reluctant to admit that a director of such distinctive talents would resort to violent sex scenes unless he had something important in mind." —Robert Denerstein, *Rocky Mountain News*, September 19, 1986

"If you combined the narrative structure and depth of characterization in *Tom Swift, Boy Detective* with several of the juicier items in Richard von Krafft-Ebing's *Psycopathia Sexualis* you'd get something a lot like, though much better than, David Lynch's *Blue Velvet*. The most appalling aspect of the entire *Blue Velvet* phenomenon, though, isn't the document itself, wretched and seamy though it may be, but the uproar raised by certain critics who've professed to see consistent humor, coherent vision, and even genius in this twisted work." —Stephen Hunter, *Baltimore Sun,* October 3, 1986

Bonnie and Clyde
1967

DIRECTOR: Arthur Penn; SCREENPLAY: David Newman, Robert Benton; CAST: Warren Beatty, Faye Dunaway, Gene Hackman, Estelle Parsons, Michael J. Pollard.

Selected to the National Film Registry, Library of Congress. Academy Award winner for Cinematography, Best Supporting Actress; nominations for Best Picture, Screenplay, Director, Actor, Actress, Supporting Actor. Winner of the New York Film Critics Circle award for Best Screenplay and the Laurel Screen Award for Drama, presented by the Writers Guild of America, West.

"It is a cheap piece of baldfaced slapstick comedy that treats the hideous depredations of that sleazy, moronic pair as though they were as full of fun and frolic as the jazz-age cut-ups in *Thoroughly Modern Millie....* This blending of farce with brutal killings is as pointless as it is lacking in taste, since it makes no valid commentary upon the already travestied truth. And it leaves an astonished critic wondering just what purpose Mr. Penn and Mr. Beatty think they serve with this strangely antique, sentimental claptrap...." —Bosley Crowther, *New York Times,* August 14, 1967

"...so incompetently written, acted, directed, and produced it would not be worth noticing were a claque not attempting to promote the idea that its sociopathology is art... There is *evil* in the *tone* of the writing, acting, and direction of this film, the calculated effect of which is to incite in the young the delusion that armed robbery and murder are mere 'happenings.'" —*Films in Review,* October 1967

Breathless (A Bout de scuffle)
1960

DIRECTOR: Jean-Luc Godard; SCREENPLAY: Jean-Luc Godard, from a story by François Truffaut; CAST: Jean-Paul Belmondo, Jean Seberg, Daniel Boulanger.

"*Breathless* upholds, and promotes, the idea that theft, murder, and amoral nihilism are legitimate reactions in contemporary society. Any society which abets such propaganda is doomed." —H. H., *Films in Review,* March 1961

Bugsy Malone
1976

DIRECTOR: Alan Parker; SCREENPLAY: Alan Parker; CAST: Scott Baio, Jodie Foster, Florrie Dugger, John Cassisi.

"What the writer-director Alan Parker has done to childhood in *Bugsy Malone* is no mere injustice.... It is an indecency, an outrage.... The film's gimmick is to turn the kids into appallingly realistic scale models of full-grown brutes and trollops for the amusement of whom, I wonder? Pederasts and child molesters, certainly, who may find something deliciously provocative about tots got up as delinquent adults.... In a world where *Bugsy Malone* can get a G rating, anything goes." —John Simon, *New York,* September 27, 1976

"A movie that is about as offensive as any I have lately seen. *Village Voice* columnist Arthur Bell has called it the 'first film for gay children.' My own feeling is that it will probably be less attractive to gay children than to pederasts." —Robert Asahina, *New Leader,* October 11, 1976

Cape Fear
1962

> DIRECTOR: J. Lee-Thompson; SCREENPLAY: James R. Webb, from the novel *The Executioners,* by John D. MacDonald; CAST: Gregory Peck, Robert Mitchum, Polly Bergen, Martin Balsam.

"The worst of life has been put on the screen to terrorize, to horrify, to make a buck....Sy Bartlett, who produced, should reflect on how socially irresponsible this picture is." —Arthur B. Clark, *Films in Review,* May 1962

The Children's Hour
1961

> DIRECTOR: William Wyler; SCREENPLAY: Lillian Hellman, from her play; CAST: Audrey Hepburn, Shirley Maclaine, James Garner, Miriam Hopkins, Fay Bainter.

"Today, when every form of perversion except masturbation and bestiality have been shown on the screen, Hellman, Wyler and the Mirisch Co. apparently thought a re-do of *The Children's Hour* would sell tickets if lesbianism were not only restored as the charge the evil child falsely brings, but also condoned....There is an explicit line of dialogue which asserts that those who choose to practice lesbianism are not destroyed by it—a claim disproved by the number of lesbians who become insane and/or commit suicide." —*Films in Review,* April 1962

A Clockwork Orange
1971 *

DIRECTOR: Stanley Kubrick; SCREENPLAY: Stanley Kubrick, from the novel by Anthony Burgess; CAST: Malcolm McDowell, Michael Bates, Adrienne Corri, Patrick Magee.
Academy Award nominations for Best Picture, Director, Screenplay.

"Literal-minded in its sex and brutality, Teutonic in its humor, Stanley Kubrick's *A Clockwork Orange* might be the work of a strict and exacting German professor who set out to make a porno-violent sci-fi comedy. Is there anything sadder—and ultimately more repellent—than a clean-minded pornographer?... How can people go on talking about the dazzling brilliance of movies and not notice that the directors are sucking up to the thugs in the audience?" —Pauline Kael, *New Yorker,* January 1, 1972

"...an evil motion picture...The way Kubrick shot and edited all this makes it obvious he is truckling to today's alienated young, and promoting the kind of nihilism that has political purposes, not all of which the young perceive. And the rest of his film is more of the same, i.e., the by-now tiresome exploitation of irrational behavior, including rape and other kinds of sadism, and murder. *All of which are condoned...*" —H.H., *Films in Review,* January 1972

The Curse of Frankenstein ———————————
1957

> DIRECTOR: Terence Fisher; SCREENPLAY: Jimmy Sangster,
> from the novel by Mary Shelley; CAST: Peter Cushing,
> Christopher Lee, Hazel Court, Robert Urquhart.

"I should rank *The Curse of Frankenstein* among the half
dozen most repulsive films I have encountered."
—C. A. Lejeune, *Observer,* May 5, 1957

The Devils ———————————————————
1970

> DIRECTOR: Ken Russell; SCREENPLAY: Ken Russell; CAST:
> Vanessa Redgrave, Oliver Reed, Dudley Sutton.

"Russell's film takes a quantum leap from his abominable
The Music Lovers into a dung heap.... Warner Brothers is
supposed to have snipped out some of the horrors,
though what they could find more odious than what they
left in defies my feeble imagination.... I shall refrain
from saying more because, not having a degree in
sanitary engineering, I don't know how to review a
cesspool." —John Simon, *New Leader,* September 6,
1971

The Dirty Dozen ———————————————
1967

> DIRECTOR: Robert Aldrich; SCREENPLAY: Nunnally Johnson,
> Lukas Heller, from the novel by E. M. Nathanson; CAST: Lee
> Marvin, Ernest Borgnine, Robert Ryan, Charles Bronson,
> Jim Brown, John Cassavetes, George Kennedy.

"...everyone connected with it should be ashamed...I
do not know enough about Producer Kenneth Hyman to

know why he should be willing to be responsible for so irresponsible a film. Director Robert Aldrich's persisting preoccupation with socially deleterious propaganda is not only limiting but ruining his career." —Gordon Drummond, *Films in Review,* August/September 1967

Dirty Harry
1971

DIRECTOR: Don Siegel; SCREENPLAY: Harry Julian Fink, Rita M. Fink, Dean Riesner; CAST: Clint Eastwood, Harry Guardino, Reni Santoni, John Vernon, John Larch, Andy Robinson.

"You could drive a truck through the plotholes in *Dirty Harry,* which wouldn't be so serious were the film not a specious, phony glorification of police and criminal brutality.... A serviceable programmer for general action audiences, plus extremists, sadists, revolutionaries, and law-and-order freaks." —*Variety,* December 22, 1971

Dressed to Kill
1980

DIRECTOR: Brian De Palma; SCREENPLAY: Brian De Palma; CAST: Michael Caine, Angie Dickinson, Nancy Allen.

"What *Dressed to Kill* dispenses liberally...is sophomoric soft-core pornography, vulgar manipulation of the emotions for mere sensation, salacious but inept dialogue that is a cross between comic-strip Freudianism and sniggering double entendres, and a plot so full of holes as to be at best a dotted line." —John Simon, *National Review,* September 19, 1980

The Exorcist
1973

DIRECTOR: William Friedkin; SCREENPLAY: William Peter
Blatty, from his novel; CAST: Ellen Burstyn, Max Von Sydow,
Linda Blair, Jason Miller.

"As for the impious thrillseekers and obscenity hounds,
have they no pride? *The Devil in Miss Jones* is one thing,
but the devil in Little Nell is quite another, devious,
craven, hypocritical way of coming by one's smut. Is
there no honor left among thieves?" —John Simon,
Esquire, April 1974

Go Naked in the World
1961

DIRECTOR: Ranald MacDougall; SCREENPLAY: Ranald
MacDougall; CAST: Gina Lollobrigida, Tony Franciosa,
Ernest Borgnine.

"Here is a film that its producer—not the censor, not
anybody else; just its producer—should have taken out
and burned.... In addition to it being unintelligent, it is
needlessly blatant and raw, full of gutter language and
trashy fake social attitudes." —Bosley Crowther, *New
York Times*, March 11, 1961

The Good, the Bad and the Ugly
1968

DIRECTOR: Sergio Leone; SCREENPLAY: Luciano Vincenzoni;
CAST: Clint Eastwood, Eli Wallach, Lee Van Cleef.

"*The Burn, the Gouge, and the Mangle* (its screen name is
simply inappropriate) must be the most expensive, pious,

and repellent movie in the history of its peculiar genre. If 42d Street is lined with little pushcarts of sadism, this film...is an entire supermarket." —Renata Adler, *New York Times,* January 25, 1968

"If one can find excuses for the commercialism of a *Doctor Doolittle,* or even a *Valley of the Dolls,* there is none whatsoever for *The Good, the Bad and the Ugly....* Crammed with sadism and a distaste for human values that would make the ordinary misanthrope seem like Pollyanna, their only possible excuse for existence is that they make money. Somehow, that isn't enough."
—Arthur Knight, *Saturday Review,* January 13, 1968

Heaven's Gate
1981

> DIRECTOR: Michael Cimino; SCREENPLAY: Michael Cimino; CAST: Kris Kristofferson, Christopher Walken, John Hurt, Sam Waterston, Brad Dourif, Isabelle Huppert, Joseph Cotten.

"One of the ugliest films I believe I have ever seen...This movie is $36 million thrown to the winds. It is the most scandalous cinematic waste I have ever seen, and remember, I've seen *Paint Your Wagon*." —Roger Ebert, *Roger Ebert's Movie Home Companion,* 1993

The Honeymoon Killers
1969

> DIRECTOR: Leonard Kastle; SCREENPLAY: Leonard Kastle; CAST: Shirley Stoler, Tony Lo Bianco, Mary Jane Higby, Doris Roberts.

"And what are we doing writing and reading about a contemptible piece of trash like *The Honeymoon*

Killers? ...They make a stunningly ugly couple in an appallingly gruesome picture which was unaccountably rated R instead of X, and we owe a great debt of ingratitude to the people who exhumed their story."
—Joseph Morgenstern, *Newsweek*, February 16, 1970

The Hunchback of Notre Dame
1939

> DIRECTOR: William Dieterle; SCREENPLAY: Sonya Levien, Bruno Frank, from the novel by Victor Hugo; CAST: Charles Laughton, Sir Cedric Hardwicke, Thomas Mitchell, Maureen O'Hara, Edmond O'Brien, Alan Marshal.

"The Music Hall is the last place in the world where we should expect to find a freak show, but *The Hunchback of Notre Dame* is that and little more....Take warning!...The film is almost unrelievedly brutal and without the saving grace of unreality which makes Frankenstein's horrors a little comic." —Frank S. Nugent, *New York Times*, January 1, 1940

I Was a Teenage Frankenstein
1957

> DIRECTOR: Herbert J. Strock; SCREENPLAY: Kenneth Langtry; CAST: Whit Bissell, Phyllis Coates, Gary Conway.

"Such films may aggravate the mass social sickness euphemistically termed 'juvenile delinquency.' ...It may be as good a time as any to raise the question of what effect this further indulgence of the cult of 'teenism' ultimately could have.... The mad doctor's assistant says 'I have no stomach for it.' That would be a plausible reaction for any adult who had read the day's headlines about teenage crime." —Richard W. Nash, *New York Times,* January 30, 1958

Lord Love a Duck
1966

DIRECTOR: George Axelrod; SCREENPLAY: Larry H. Johnson, George Axelrod; CAST: Roddy McDowall, Tuesday Weld, Lola Albright, Ruth Gordon.

"...about the most revolting piece of draff the smoker-room of George (*Paris When It Sizzles*) Axelrod has yet produced. It is amateurish, excessive, pornographic, illiterate, and—worse—unoriginal....The actors are allowed...to wallow in excesses that would embarrass the Three Stooges...." —Rex Reed, from his collection *Big Screen, Little Screen,* 1971

Love Me Tender
1956

DIRECTOR: Robert D. Webb; SCREENPLAY: Robert Buckner; CAST: Richard Egan, Debra Paget, Elvis Presley.

"*Love Me Tender* will have no place in motion picture history, but it may very well have a place in the history of American morals and mores, for Presley is a pied piper who could lead his followers to an end more socially deleterious than their permanent disappearance in a cave." —Henry Hart, *Films in Review,* December 1956

Mahler
1975

DIRECTOR: Ken Russell; SCREENPLAY: Ken Russell; CAST:
Robert Powell, Georgina Hale, Richard Morant.

"Collectors of supreme cinematic monstrosities had better keep a sharp lookout for Ken Russell's latest.... The
film is in such demented and rotten taste that I do not
wish to waste much space on it." —John Simon, *Esquire,*
April 1975

"A discombobulated, flatulent film...Overripe, hyper-
bolic, hysterical..." —Jay Cocks, *Time,* May 17, 1976

Night of the Living Dead
1968

DIRECTOR: George A. Romero; SCREENPLAY: John A. Russo;
CAST: Judith O'Dea, Russell Streiner, Duane Jones, Karl
Hardman, Keith Wayne.

"Until the Supreme Court establishes clearcut guidelines
for the pornography of violence, *Night of the Living Dead*
will serve nicely as an outer-limit definition by example.
In a mere 90 minutes, this horror film (pun intended)
casts serious aspersions on the integrity and social responsibility of its Pittsburgh-based makers, distrib Walter Reade, the film industry as a whole, and exhibs who
book the pic, as well as raising doubts about the future of
the regional cinema movement and about the moral
health of filmgoers who cheerfully opt for this unre-
lieved orgy of sadism." —*Variety,* October 16, 1968

Pat Garrett and Billy the Kid _____
1973

DIRECTOR: Sam Peckinpah; SCREENPLAY: Rudolph Wurlitzer;
CAST: James Coburn, Kris Kristofferson, Bob Dylan.

"...due to the vagaries of our laws and national morality
it is possible for children to accompany their parents or
other adults to see *Pat Garrett and Billy the Kid,* and that, I
submit, is truly an obscene notion...It is the ultimate
obscenity, because it corrupts in the name of entertainment, and because we allow children to see it and
congratulate ourselves because they can't after all see
movies like *Deep Throat.*"   —Michael Korda, *Glamour,*
June 1973

The Phantom of the Opera _____
1925

DIRECTOR: Rupert Julien; SCREENPLAY: Raymond Shrock,
Elliot Clawson, from the novel by Gaston Leroux; CAST: Lon
Chaney, Mary Philbin, Norman Kerry, Snitz Edwards, Bigson
Gowland.

"...probably the greatest inducement to nightmare that
has yet been screened...It's impossible to believe there
are a majority of picturegoers who prefer this revolting
sort of a tale on the screen."   —*Variety,* September 9,
1925

Pretty Baby _____
1978

DIRECTOR: Louis Malle; SCREENPLAY: Polly Platt, Louis Malle;
CAST: Keith Carradine, Susan Sarandon, Brooke Shields.

In a New Orleans bordello: Brooke Shields and Susan Sarandon in *Pretty Baby*

"I feel that Brooke Shields, when she rivets her step-father and the audience with that penetrating stare in the final sequence, is really looking through and beyond the poor fools who paid four dollars in the hope of seeing a 12-year-old do a nude love scene. She is really looking at Louis Malle, Polly Platt and Paramount Pictures, who are trying to tell us the story of her degradation when their own is so obvious in every frame. And perhaps she is even looking beyond them to each of us in a society that makes such exploitation possible."
—Richard A. Blake, *America*, April 22, 1978

The Producers
1968

> DIRECTOR: Mel Brooks; SCREENPLAY: Mel Brooks; CAST: Zero Mostel, Gene Wilder, Kenneth Mars.

"This film was written and directed by Mel Brooks, so the responsibility is clearly fixed. It seemed to me an almost flawless triumph of bad taste, unredeemed by charm or style.... *The Producers* is warmly recommended for all those who regard the following things as hilarious: Hitler, queers, hysterics, old ladies being pawed, and infantilism." —Arthur Schlesinger Jr., *Vogue*, February 15, 1968

"For myself, I couldn't find in the proceedings even a wild caricature of anything recognizably human, and my mind boggled at the psychological implications in the premise that any audience would laugh at the play within the movie." —Moira Walsh, *America*, April 6, 1968

Psycho
1960

DIRECTOR: Alfred Hitchcock; SCREENPLAY: Joseph Stefano,
from the novel by Robert Bloch; CAST: Anthony Perkins,
Vera Miles, John Gavin, Janet Leigh.

"...puts you in the position of rubbernecking at the
horrors of the diseased mind; it makes you feel un-
clean...In *Psycho,* Hitchcock is not an entertainer, but a
pander of vicarious perversion....It is incumbent on us
to inspect the real horrors of our time, but we don't have
to traffic with Hitchcock's giggling obscenities."
—Robert Hatch, *Nation,* July 2, 1960

"At close range, the camera watches every twitch, gurgle,
convulsion, and hemorrhage in the process by which a
living human being becomes a corpse....Director Hitchcock bears down too heavily in this one, and the delicate
illusion of reality necessary for a creak-and-shriek movie
becomes, instead, a spectacle of stomach-churning horror." —*Time,* June 27, 1960

Repulsion
1965

DIRECTOR: Roman Polanski; SCREENPLAY: Roman Polanski,
Gerard Brach; CAST: Catherine Deneuve, Ian Hendry, John
Fraser.

"...horrors fondled for the camera...it is certainly rele-
vant to our position in the audience to ask the simple,
basic, 'Why was this movie made?'" —Pauline Kael,
Vogue, December 1965

"...one leaves the cinema feeling bruised and soiled."
—H.H., *Christian Science Monitor,* June 30, 1965

The Road Warrior
1981 (also known as *Mad Max II*)

DIRECTOR: George Miller; SCREENPLAY: Terry Hayes, George Miller, Brian Hannant; CAST: Mel Gibson, Bruce Spence, Vernon Wells, Emil Minty.

"It's bad enough to encounter the fascist mentality and ugly violence of George Miller's new film, *The Road Warrior*. But even more disturbing is the way an army of movie critics have hopped on the picture's bandwagon, eagerly praising its lurid images and slam-bang style." — David Sterritt, *Christian Science Monitor*, September 2, 1982

Sid and Nancy
1986

DIRECTOR: Alex Cox; SCREENPLAY: Alex Cox, Abbe Wool; CAST: Gary Oldman, Chloe Webb.

"A film so depressing it makes you want to kill yourself...makes Lynch's *Blue Velvet* look like a re-run of *Ozzie and Harriet*...President Reagan has declared war on drugs....He'll need an oxygen tank to get through *Sid and Nancy*." —Rex Reed, *New York Post*, October 3, 1986

Spencer's Mountain
1963

DIRECTOR: Delmer Daves; SCREENPLAY: Delmer Daves; CAST: Henry Fonda, Maureen O'Hara, James MacArthur, Donald Crisp, Wally Cox.

"...for sheer prurience and perverted morality disguised as piety makes the nudie shows at the Rialto look like Walt Disney productions...Outstanding for its smirking sexuality, its glorification of the vulgar, its patronizing tone toward the humble, its mealymouthed piety..." —Judith Crist, *New York Herald Tribune*, May 19, 1963

Splendor in the Grass
1961

> DIRECTOR: Elia Kazan; SCREENPLAY: William Inge; CAST: Natalie Wood, Warren Beatty, Pat Hingle.

"Kazan may have spent two years trying, but he has not gotten it right. Once again the hatred of American life he puts into his films results in caricatures. In fact, some of the scenes in *Splendor in the Grass* are so repulsive they seem deliberately calculated to denigrate the US in foreign eyes." —Arthur B. Clark, *Films in Review*, November 1961

Straw Dogs
1971

> DIRECTOR: Sam Peckinpah; SCREENPLAY: David Zelag Goodman, Sam Peckinpah, from the novel *The Siege of Trencher's Farm*, by Gordon M. Williams; CAST: Dustin Hoffman, Susan George, Peter Vaughan, David Warner, T. P. McKenna, Colin Welland.

"...just a gang of mental defectives slaughtering each other and raping a very rapable girl in a vast variety of blood-soaked sadistic and perverse ways, without pause and without purpose...(All anyone with an IQ of 70-plus can get out of this film is a case of the heaves.)" —Judith Crist, *New York*, January 24, 1972

"I would have walked out of *Straw Dogs* if I'd been anything but a professional critic." —Gary Arnold, *Washington Post,* January 10, 1972

Tea and Sympathy
1956

> DIRECTOR: Vincente Minnelli; SCREENPLAY: Robert Anderson, from his play; CAST: Deborah Kerr, John Kerr, Leif Erickson.

"At its best *Tea and Sympathy* is an inferior Candida, and, at its worst, pernicious propaganda for sexual degeneracy." —Veronica Hume, *Films in Review,* November 1956

The Texas Chainsaw Massacre
1974

> DIRECTOR: Tobe Hooper; SCREENPLAY: Tobe Hooper, Kim Henkel; CAST: Marilyn Burns, Allen Danziger, Paul A. Partain, William Vail.

"...a despicable film... Torture and gruesome death through a filtered lens are still ugly and obscene.... Craziness handled without sensitivity is a degrading, senseless misuse of film and time." —Linda Gross, *Los Angeles Times,* October 30, 1974

"The less said about Tobe Hooper's *The Texas Chainsaw Massacre* the better.... The fact that it is rather efficiently and effectively done only makes the film more unpalatable." —*London Times,* November 19, 1976

Thunderbolt and Lightfoot _____
1974

> DIRECTOR: Michael Cimino; SCREENPLAY: Michael Cimino;
> CAST: Clint Eastwood, Jeff Bridges, George Kennedy.
> Academy Award nomination for Best Actor (Jeff Bridges).

"A demented exercise in Hollywood hackery...Cheap
potboilers like this shouldn't be released. They should be
recycled and used to catch droppings on the floors of
chicken coops." —Rex Reed, *New York Daily News,*
May 24, 1974

"...degrades everyone and everything it touches, including the genre of the caper film, which serves as the
vehicle for this voyeuristic appeal to youthful preoccupation with sex, cars and violence..." —*Christian Century,*
May 22, 1974

Two for the Road _____
1966

> DIRECTOR: Stanley Donen; SCREENPLAY: Frederic Raphael;
> CAST: Albert Finney, Audrey Hepburn.
> Academy Award nomination for Best Screenplay.

"I have long believed soapera (soap opera) is so stultify-
ing intellectually and emotionally it is culturally im-
moral, and that when it's hopped up to make it appeal to
'sophisticates' it's even more so. I also believe that when,
as *Two for the Road* does, it presents adultery as a matter-
of-course peccadillo, it's anti-social as well. Be this as it
may, *Two for the Road* is soapera for sophisticates with
Audrey Hepburn prostituting her very genuine acting
abilities on behalf of a script designed by Frederic

Raphael exclusively for feeble female minds." —Flavia
Wharton, *Films in Review,* May 1967

Wild at Heart
1990

> DIRECTOR: David Lynch; SCREENPLAY: David Lynch; CAST:
> Nicolas Cage, Laura Dern, Diane Ladd, Willem Dafoe,
> Isabella Rossellini, Harry Dean Stanton, Crispin Glover.
> Winner of the Palme d'Or from the 1990 Cannes Film
> Festival.

"From the opening scene of *Wild at Heart,* David Lynch
crosses the line between art and obscenity. A white man
beats a black man to a literal pulp...This knock-down-
and-drag-out is an epic battle of the races. Not only does
the white man win; in Lynch's view, he *should* win....His
vision coheres around the self-centeredness (and racism)
that signifies bad art." —Armond White, *City Sun,*
August 22, 1990

The Wild Bunch
1969

> DIRECTOR: Sam Peckinpah; SCREENPLAY: Walon Green, Sam
> Peckinpah; CAST: William Holden, Ernest Borgnine, Robert
> Ryan, Edmond O'Brien, Warren Oates.
> Academy Award nominations for Best Screenplay, Score.

"If you hate bloodshed and corruption, you're in trouble,
pal...and you will never make friends of Sam Peckinpah
fans. Well, Sam Peckinpah fans, I say up yours. *The Wild
Bunch* stinks and I don't care who knows it. This is the
most pretentious, most violent blood-letting it has ever

been my grave misfortune to witness on a motion picture screen...." —Rex Reed, from his collection *Big Screen, Little Screen,* 1971

"...contains not one but two (count 'em) massacres violent and gory enough to make a Caligula puke.... Technically *The Wild Bunch* is a masterpiece; ethically, it's a monstrosity....What Stalin or Hitler could have conceived a more stunning paean to death than Peckinpah's visual descent into hell?" —Sherwood Ross, *Christian Century,* August 20, 1969

"Though *The Wild Bunch* has its vociferous supporters, it also has its outraged critics who think, as I do myself, that it is just the wrong picture at the wrong time and that, whatever its intentions, any purported constructive impact is obliterated in a sea of blood." —Moira Walsh, *America,* July 19, 1969

"I would prefer to believe that Sam Peckinpah...was sincere when he stated that he wanted to make a picture so strong, so stomach-churning, so detailed in its catalogue of horrors that all the glamour, all the attraction of violence for its own sake would promptly disappear. I think he is wrong, but I very much doubt that anyone who was not totally honest in his wrongheadedness could ever come up with a picture as wholly revolting as this." —Arthur Knight, *Saturday Review,* July 5, 1969

The World of Suzie Wong
1960

DIRECTOR: Richard Quine; SCREENPLAY: John Patrick, from the play by Paul Osborn; CAST: William Holden, Nancy Kwan, Sylvia Syms.

"What ignorance of Hong Kong whores, what cultural illiteracy! Not even fascinating color photography of Hong Kong itself, and the performance of the lovely Sylvia Syms as the spurned English girl, atone for the amorality and commercial venality of this ridiculous film." —Adelaide Comerford, *Films in Review,* December 1960

7

Were They Really That Bad? ____

Savage Overreactions to Good *Movies*

Alice Doesn't Live Here Anymore _____
1974

DIRECTOR: Martin Scorsese; SCREENPLAY: Robert Getchell;
CAST: Ellen Burstyn, Alfred Lutter, Kris Kristofferson,
Diane Ladd, Harvey Keitel, Jodie Foster.

Academy Award for Best Actress; nominations for
Screenplay, Supporting Actress.

"...the film has a heart conceivably bigger than a bread
box, but a brain surely smaller than a bread crumb."
—John Simon, from his collection *Reverse Angle*, 1982

Alice's Restaurant _____
1969

DIRECTOR: Arthur Penn; SCREENPLAY: Venable Herndon,
Arthur Penn; CAST: Arlo Guthrie, Pat Quinn, James
Broderick.

Academy Award nomination for Best Director.

"…a formless, pointless, plotless piece of trash directed by Arthur Penn, who should know better… The acting is uniformly nauseating and so is the picture. You don't have to actually eat in Alice's Restaurant to get ptomaine; just see the movie." —Rex Reed, from his collection *Big Screen, Little Screen,* 1971

Amarcord
1973

DIRECTOR: Federico Fellini; SCREENPLAY: Federico Fellini, Tonino Guerra; CAST: Puppela Maggio, Magali Noel, Armando Brancia.
Academy Award winner for Best Foreign Film; nominations for Screenplay, Director.

"Rather than stopping at 'I Remember,' Fellini's title should have gone on: 'I Remember, I Reuse, I Rereuse, Until I Don't Even Remember What It Is I Am Rereusing.'…Everything in the film has either been done before by Fellini, in many cases more than once, or else it wasn't worth doing in the first place." —John Simon, *Esquire,* December 1974

"I cannot look on *Amarcord* as anything but further evidence that Federico Fellini runs a lively risk of becoming the cinema's most eminent bore….I feel that a dotard (Fellini is a bit my junior) has clawed onto my elbow in order to gabble a lot of unrelated local yarns to the accompanying cackle of malicious laughter." —Robert Hatch, *Nation,* October 12, 1974

Apocalypse Now
1979

DIRECTOR: Francis Ford Coppola; SCREENPLAY: John Milius, Francis Ford Coppola; CAST: Martin Sheen, Robert Duvall, Frederic Forrest, Marlon Brando, Dennis Hopper.

Academy Award winner for Cinematography; nominations for Best Picture, Screenplay, Director, Supporting Actor. Winner of the British Academy of Film and Television Arts awards for Director, Supporting Actor; the Palme d'Or from the Cannes Film Festival; Golden Globe winner for Director, Score, Supporting Actor.

"It is not so much an epic account of a grueling war as an incongruous, extravagant monument to artistic self-defeat.... Yet, lest we lose our perspective in contemplating this disappointing effort, it should be remembered that the failure of an ambitious $30 million film is not a tragedy. The Viet Nam War was a tragedy. *Apocalypse Now* is but this decade's most extraordinary Hollywood folly." —Frank Rich, *Time*, August 27, 1979

"The atmosphere of Francis Ford Coppola's lamentable magnum opus, *Apocalypse Now,* a ruinously pretentious and costly allegorical epic about war in Vietnam, recalls nothing so much as the notorious campfire scene in Mel Brooks's *Blazing Saddles.* It's the cumulative effect generated by mixing richly portentous imagery with absurdly portentous prose, starkly portentous sound, and flatulently portentous music." —Gary Arnold, *Washington Post,* October 3, 1979

"*Apocalypse Now* stinks. After years of work and the expenditure of multiple millions of dollars, director Francis Ford Coppola has brought forth a very ugly, very minor work." —Scott Cain, *Atlanta Journal,* October 12, 1979

Au Revoir, Les Enfants
1988

DIRECTOR: Louis Malle; SCREENPLAY: Louis Malle; CAST:
Gaspard Manesse, Raphaël Fejtö, Francine Racette.
Academy Award nomination for Best Foreign Film.

"He nailed the big scene, I'll give him that. The pity is
that imagination deserted him, and that he couldn't
build a freer, more daring, less hackneyed film around it.
It seems almost a waste of good kindling." —David
Edelstein, *Village Voice*, February 23, 1988

L'Avventura
1961

DIRECTOR: Michelangelo Antonioni; SCREENPLAY:
Michelangelo Antonioni, Elio Bartolini, Tonino Guerra;
CAST: Monica Vitti, Lea Massari, Gabriele Ferzetti.

"The international clacque that has been organized on
behalf of this amateurish motion picture reminds me of
the people who cried out against the child who said the
king had no clothes. This film is a fraud.... The simple
truth is Antonioni had no script, is not fertile at im-
provisation, and having produced a quantity of meaningless footage, has been so conscienceless as to go along
with his producer's efforts to palm it all off as art."
—Ellen Fitzpatrick, *Films in Review*, May 1961

The Birds
1963

DIRECTOR: Alfred Hitchcock; SCREENPLAY: Evan Hunter,
from a story by Daphne Du Maurier; CAST: Rod Taylor,
Tippi Hedren, Jessica Tandy, Suzanne Pleshette.

"The script by Evan Hunter...is absolutely bereft of even
the slick-magazine sophistication that Hitchcock's films
usually have. The dialogue is stupid, the characters
insuffienctly developed to rank as cliches, the story
incohesive....Suzanne Pleshette as a local schoolteacher
is unobjectionable. The rest of the cast are offensively
bad." —Stanley Kauffmann, *New Republic*, April 13,
1963

Blade Runner ————————————————————
1982

> DIRECTOR: Ridley Scott; SCREENPLAY: Hampton Fancher,
> David People, from the novel *Do Androids Dream of Electric
> Sheep?*, by Philip K. Dick; CAST: Harrison Ford, Rutger
> Hauer, Sean Young.
>
> Selected to the National Film Registry, Library of
> Congress. Academy Award nominations for Art Direction,
> Visual Effects.

"To put it briefly, scientifically and charitably, this is a
very feverish view of life a mere 37 years, from now.
Some of you readers will still be alive and suffering then,
so be warned....The kids may be able to swallow this
stuff without gagging." —Archer Winsten, *New York
Post,* June 25, 1982

"The sets are indeed impressive...but they are no com-
pensation for a narrative so lame that it seems in need of
a wheelchair." —Tom Milne, *Monthly Film Bulletin,*
September 1982

Blow-Up
1966

DIRECTOR: Michelangelo Antonioni; SCREENPLAY:
Michelangelo Antonioni; CAST: David Hemmings, Sarah
Miles, Vanessa Redgrave.

Academy Award nominations for Best Director,
Screenplay. Grand Prix winner at the Cannes Film Festival.

"The only explosive thing about *Blow-Up* is the title.
Otherwise it is just another exercise in petrifying
boredom, from Italy's Nihilist director Michelangelo
Antonioni.... It is spoken in English, but in any language
in the world it has the unmistakable sound of a big fat
yawn." —Rex Reed, from his collection *Big Screen, Little
Screen,* 1971

Cactus Flower
1969

DIRECTOR: Gene Saks; SCREENPLAY: I. A. L. Diamond, from
the play by Abe Burrows; CAST: Ingrid Bergman, Walter
Matthau, Goldie Hawn.

Academy Award winner for Best Supporting Actress
(Goldie Hawn).

"As a play it wasn't much, but as a movie it's a hopeless
disaster in which absolutely nothing goes right....*Cactus
Flower* has no feel, no style, no tempo, no rhythm."
—Rex Reed, *Holiday,* November 1969

Carrie
1976

DIRECTOR: Brian De Palma; SCREENPLAY: Laurence D.
Cohen, from the novel by Stephen King; CAST: Sissy Spacek,
Piper Laurie, Amy Irving, William Katt, John Travolta.

Academy Award nominations for Best Actress (Sissy
Spacek), Supporting Actress (Piper Laurie).

"...a supremely silly movie about nothing at all...Per-
haps I'm more of a purist than I ever realized. I like
horror films that keep me on the edge of my seat. A
horror film that lulls me to the edge of sleep is innova-
tive, all right, but in the wrong way.... For any one except
the film buff, *Carrie* is a waste of time." —Vincent
Canby, *New York Times,* December 5, 1976

"Pandering to the most base level of popular taste has
long been business-as-usual in Hollywood. New and
substantial proof of that truism comes with *Carrie,* a
shallow, nasty-minded, extremely bloody picture....the
only ones who stand a chance of coming out ahead,
where shamelessly exploitive movies like *Carrie* are concerned, are the money men behind the project. The
thrills get cheaper all the time, but not the price of
admission." —Susan Stark, *Detroit Free Press,* November
16, 1976

"King endowed Carrie with telekinesis so that she could
be an instrument for expressing what I interpret as his
own undying hatred of young people, high-school students in particular. As portrayed by adapter Lawrence
D. Cohen and director Brian De Palma, King's high-
school students are the most repulsive young people to
appear on the screen since the youth films of the late

Sixties. And that includes Carrie herself." —R. H. Gardner, *Baltimore Sun,* November 8, 1976

A Clockwork Orange ————————————————
1971

DIRECTOR: Stanley Kubrick; SCREENPLAY: Stanley Kubrick, from the novel by Anthony Burgess; CAST: Malcolm McDowell, Michael Bates, Adrienne Corri, Patrick Magee.

Academy Award nominations for Best Picture, Director, Screenplay.

"...a painless, bloodless, and ultimately pointless futuristic fantasy...See *A Clockwork Orange* for yourself and suffer the damnation of boredom....What we,have here is simply a pretentious fake." —Andrew Sarris, *Village Voice,* December 30, 1971

"Something has gone seriously wrong with the talented Kubrick. I won't hazard guesses as to what it is. But the one thing that, two films ago, I'd never have thought possible to say about a Kubrick film is true of *A Clockwork Orange*: it's boring." —Stanley Kauffmann, *New Republic,* January 1, 1972

The Conversation ————————————————
1974

DIRECTOR: Francis Ford Coppola; SCREENPLAY: Francis Ford Coppola; CAST: Gene Hackman, John Cazale, Allen Garfield, Frederic Forrest, Cindy Williams, Teri Garr, Harrison Ford, Robert Duvall.

Academy Award nominations for Best Picture, Screenplay.

"Coppola...among a group of particularly self-conscious directors, is arguable the most self-conscious. His continual preference for the big idea over the small detail is undermined by his intellectual superficiality. And when he focuses on his themes with the unrelenting seriousness of tone and style of *The Conversation,* the result is more gimmicky than thoughtful." —Jon Landau, *Rolling Stone,* May 23, 1974

Day for Night (*La Nuit américaine*) ————————
1973

> DIRECTOR: François Truffaut; SCREENPLAY: François Truffaut, Jean-Louis Richard, Suzanne Schiffman; CAST: Jacqueline Bisset, Valentina Cortese, Jean-Pierre Aumont, Jean-Pierre Léaud.
>
> Academy Award winner for Best Foreign Film; nominations for Screenplay, Director, Supporting Actress.

"*Day for Night* is a movie for the movie-struck, the essentially naive—those who would rather see a movie, any movie (a bad one, a stupid one, or an evanescent, sweet-but-dry little wafer of a movie, like this one), than do anything else. It's for those (one meets them on campuses) who can say 'I love all movies.' It's not for someone like me, who can walk out on *A Touch of Class* without a twinge." —Pauline Kael, *New Yorker,* October 15, 1973

Dead Ringers ————————————————————
1988

> DIRECTOR: David Cronenberg; SCREENPLAY: David Cronenberg, Norman Snider, from the book *Twins* by Barry Wood; CAST: Jeremy Irons, Genevieve Bujold, Heidi von Paleske, Barbara Gordon.

"...like a piece of salami at the end of a year in the refrigerator—long, cold, hard and smelly..." —Stephen Hunter, *Baltimore Sun,* September 23, 1988

"...a beautifully crafted dud...Despite some sardonic verbal and visual jokes, the extraordinary flim-flammery that allowed Irons to act with himself, and the spectral glow of the sets and costumes...*Dead Ringers* is really dead." —Michael Sragow, *San Francisco Examiner,* September 23, 1988

The Dead Zone
1983

> DIRECTOR: David Cronenberg; SCREENPLAY: Jeffrey Boam, from the novel by Stephen King; CAST: Christopher Walken, Brooke Adams, Tom Skerritt, Herbert Lom, Anthony Zerbe, Colleen Dewhurst.

"...a grade B movie made with big stars. The question is just why do we need still another film about (low ominous tones here) 'psychic phenomena?' Try greed, try Stephen King's big bucks success...There's a telling line about halfway through when Johnny complains to his doctor: 'When the spells come, it feels like I'm dying inside.' The corpse is the movie." —Roxanne T. Mueller, *Cleveland Plain Dealer,* October 24, 1983

"As in all of Cronenberg's work, there's something slightly sick about *The Dead Zone,* even though its protagonist takes a courageous moral stand in the end. The Canadian director's attempts at black humor fall flat and undermine the movie's credibility....*The Dead Zone,* like Walken's character, suffers, from brain damage." —Dennis Fiely, *Columbus Evening Dispatch,* October 25, 1983

"The most extraordinary thing about *The Dead Zone* is how terribly ordinary it is. David Cronenberg, creator of such surreal cinematic nightmares as *Videodrome* and *Scanners,* is credited as director. And that's the only shocking thing about this flaccid thriller.... It is as indifferently written and directed as a second-rate TV movie." —Joe Leydon, *Houston Post,* October 25, 1983

"A first-class cast strikes out. Although Christopher Walken is a pretty convincing psychic-freak, pitching Johnny somewhere to the left of a somnambulist, the evil politician totally eludes Martin Sheen.... Brooke Adams, Tom Skerritt, Herbert Lom, Anthony Zerbe and Colleen Dewhurst parade by, untaxed, in inconsequential bits. By actual count, there is one surprise...but otherwise, you're a good two scenes ahead of the film all the way. The déjà vu is deadly." —Harry Haun, *New York Daily News,* October 21, 1983

Death in Venice ——————————————————
1971

> DIRECTOR: Luchino Visconti; SCREENPLAY: Luchino Visconti, Nicola Bandalucco, from the novel by Thomas Mann; CAST: Dirk Bogarde, Bjorn Andresen, Silvana Mangano, Marisa Berenson.

"Instead of bringing the story to life, Visconti has, I'm afraid, embalmed it." —Vincent Canby, *New York Times,* June 18, 1971

"This movie is a unique insult: it is a travesty of the work of two of the most beloved artists of the early twentieth century—Thomas Mann and Gustav Mahler." —David Denby, *Atlantic,* September 1971

The Deer Hunter
1978

DIRECTOR: Michael Cimino; SCREENPLAY: Deric Washburn;
CAST: Robert De Niro, Christopher Walken, John Cazale,
John Savage, Meryl Streep.

Academy Award winner for Best Picture, Director,
Supporting Actor (Christopher Walken); nominations for
Screenplay, Cinematography, Actor, Supporting Actress.

"Try to imagine a boneless elephant sitting in your lap
for three hours while you're trying to think. It's flabby
beyond belief, convinced not only of its importance but
of its relevance to Americans (i.e. human beings) everywhere.... If only we could send this heavy gray lump off
to school, or at least get it a respectable job in the
circus." —Jonathan Rosenbaum, *Take One*, March 1979

The Devil and Daniel Webster (also known as *Here Is a Man, All That Money Can Buy*)
1941

DIRECTOR: William Dieterle; SCREENPLAY: Dan Totheroh,
from the story by Stephen Vincent Benet; CAST: Walter
Huston, James Craig, Anne Shirley, Simone Simon, Edward
Arnold.

Academy Award for Best Score; nomination for Best
Actor (Walter Huston).

"Theatre operators will have to be magicians to make
this one stand up before any but the most naive type of
audiences....it is a very bad screenplay, not helped by
Dieterle's slow-paced direction." —*Variety*, July 16, 1941

Dr. Jekyll and Mr. Hyde
1941

DIRECTOR: Victor Fleming; SCREENPLAY: John Lee Mahin;
CAST: Spencer Tracy, Ingrid Bergman, Lana Turner.

"…preposterous mixture of hokum and high-flown psychological balderdash…a Grand Guignol chiller with
delusions of grandeur, a nightmare interpreted by a
reader of tea leaves, a mulligan stew hidden under an
expensive souffle." —Theodore Strauss, *New York
Times,* August 13, 1941

East of Eden
1955

DIRECTOR: Elia Kazan; SCREENPLAY: Paul Osborn, from the
novel by John Steinbeck; CAST: Raymond Massey, James
Dean, Julie Harris, Dick Davalos, Jo Van Fleet, Burl Ives,
Albert Dekker.

Academy Award winner for Best Supporting Actress (Jo
Van Fleet); nominations for Screenplay, Director, Supporting
Actor (James Dean).

"Under the direction of Elia Kazan, *East of Eden* offers a
new wrinkle in CinemaScope. Not only is the screen as
wide as California but the camera angles are frequently
distorted. This is unsettling enough, but it is the acting
that will really get you down." —John McCarten, *New
Yorker,* March 19, 1955

"…sprawling, lurid, old-fashioned, generally unaffect-
ing . . ." —Lee Rogow, *Saturday Review,* March 19, 1955

The Elephant Man
1980

DIRECTOR: David Lynch; SCREENPLAY: Christopher de Vore, Eric Bergren, David Lynch; CAST: Anthony Hopkins, John Hurt, John Gielgud, Anne Bancroft.

Academy Award nominations for Best Picture, Screenplay, Director, Editing, Art Direction, Costume Design. Winner of the British Academy of Film and Television Arts awards for Best Film, Actor, Production Design.

"*The Elephant Man* is a thoroughly bad movie.... The story which needs tact and taste in the telling, was, unfortunately, produced by Mel Brooks, not known for either.... Wild elephants shouldn't drag you to this one." —John Simon, *National Review*, January 23, 1981

Field of Dreams
1989

DIRECTOR: Phil Alden Robinson; SCREENPLAY: Phil Alden Robinson, from the book *Shoeless Joe*, by W. P. Kinsella; CAST: Kevin Costner, Amy Madigan, James Earl Jones, Ray Liotta, Burt Lancaster, Timothy Busfield.

Academy Award nominations for Best Picture, Adapted Screenplay, Original Score.

"If *Field of Dreams* doesn't put a softball-sized lump in your throat, it's not exactly unproductive either. Watch where you put your feet, Shoeless Joe. There's enough horseshit here to fertilize Ray's farm, the rest of the county, and Iowa, too." —J. Hoberman, *Village Voice*, April 25, 1989

The 400 Blows (*Les Quatre cents coups*) —————
1959

> DIRECTOR: François Truffaut; SCREENPLAY: François Truffaut;
> CAST: Jean-Pierre Leaud, Claire Maurier, Albert Remy.
> Academy Award nomination for Best Screenplay.

"Considerable art is required to animate such cliché
script situations and character motivations. No such art
is visible here. The all-important boy-actor (Jean-Pierre
Leaud) is not too appealing....Truffaut's direction is
amateur." —Louise Corbin, *Films in Review,* November
1959

The Group —————
1966

> DIRECTOR: Sidney Lumet; SCREENPLAY: Sidney Buchman,
> from the novel by Mary McCarthy; CAST: Joanna Pettet,
> Candice Bergen, Jessica Walter, Joan Hackett, Elizabeth
> Hartman, Larry Hagman, Hal Holbrook.

"...if it is seriously intended—it is the worst misfire of a
movie in many a year...it is so awkwardly and mawkishly
played that it seems not only a travesty of the nineteen-
thirties but an insult to a generation of human
beings." —Bosley Crowther, *New York Times,* March 17,
1966

Harry and Tonto —————
1974

> DIRECTOR: Paul Mazursky; SCREENPLAY: Paul Mazursky, Josh
> Greenfield; CAST: Art Carney, Ellen Burstyn, Chief Dan
> George, Geraldine Fitzgerald.

Academy Award winner for Best Actor (Art Carney); nomination for Best Screenplay.

"That insufferably cute and crass filmmaker Paul Mazursky is back with *Harry and Tonto,* in which a much abused New York senior citizen packs up his beloved cat and heads west.... the whole thing is rife with Mazursky's maniacal striving to fuse the offbeat and the slick into the indigestible... The cat acts best, and with condign condescension." —John Simon, *Esquire,* November 1974

Harvey
1951

DIRECTOR: Henry Koster; SCREENPLAY: Mary Chase (with Oscar Brodney), from her play; CAST: James Stewart, Josephine Hull, Victoria Horne, Peggy Dow, Cecil Kellaway, Jesse White.

Academy Award for Best Supporting Actress (Josephine Hull); nomination for Best Actor (James Stewart).

"...a whimsey that is just around Pooh corner, from mawkishness...Stewart is O.K., and that is about the size of it.... He walks through *Harvey* with no trouble and, I think, without taking any. At least he never succeeds in evoking the presence of his invisible pal." —Robert Hatch, *New Republic,* January 15, 1951

The Heartbreak Kid
1972

DIRECTOR: Elaine May; SCREENPLAY: Neil Simon; CAST: Charles Grodin, Cybill Shepherd, Jeannie Berlin, Eddie Albert.

Academy Award nominations for Best Supporting Actress (Jeannie Berlin), Supporting Actor (Eddie Albert).

"*The Heartbreak Kid* is the latest in a relatively new kind of American film comedy—glittery trash. Most of these pictures come from Neil Simon, who wrote this one, or his imitators....this film is meretricious, stone-fingered and unbelievable, all done with a smart-ass tone that is supposed to make us think it's comically candid. Simon and May have just found new tinsel wrappings for trash." —Stanley Kauffmann, *New Republic,* January 6–13, 1973

Hiroshima, Mon Amour
1959

> DIRECTOR: Alain Resnais; SCREENPLAY: Marguerite Duras; CAST: Emmanuele Riva, Eiji Okada.
> Academy Award nomination for Best Screenplay.

"That a film so amateur should receive so much critical acclaim is a sad commentary on the state of Western culture....the enthusiasm of a-political critics for this picture reveals a mental confusion so close to intellectual bankruptcy as to alarm everyone who believes the West *has* a mission." —H.H., *Films in Review,* June/July 1960

Hud
1963

> DIRECTOR: Martin Ritt; SCREENPLAY: Irving Ravetch, Harriet Frank, from a novel by Larry McMurtry; CAST: Paul Newman, Patricia Neal, Melvyn Douglas, Brandon de Wilde.
> Academy Award winner for Cinematography, Best Supporting Actor (Melvyn Douglas), Supporting Actress (Patricia Neal); nominations for Screenplay, Director, Actor.

"Hud swaggers across the screen like Evil Incarnate, but his assorted peccadilloes barely fill the quota of a Peck's Bad Boy of the Prairie....Frankly, I thought the real villain of *Hud* was the self-righteous father, possibly because Melvyn Douglas gave the worst performance." —Andrew Sarris, *Village Voice,* June 27, 1963

I Was a Male War Bride
1949

> DIRECTOR: Howard Hawks; SCREENPLAY: Charles Lederer, Hagar Wilde, Leonard Spigelgass; CAST: Cary Grant, Ann Sheridan, Marion Marshall.

"A bedroom farce with a scattering of laughs which are muffled by as thick a mixture of stale crumbs and old chestnuts as Hollywood has ever stuffed into a high-priced turkey." —*Time,* September 12, 1949

Invasion of the Body Snatchers
1978

> DIRECTOR: Philip Kaufman; SCREENPLAY: W. D. Richter; CAST: Donald Sutherland, Brooke Adams, Leonard Nimoy, Veronica Cartwright, Jeff Goldblum, Kevin McCarthy, Don Siegel.

"I suppose not much should have been expected, from the writer of *Nickleodeon* or the director of *The Great Northfield Minnesota Raid.* In fact, the real trouble with *Invasion of the Body Snatchers* is that it was made by the same pod people it is supposed to be about." —Robert Asahina, *New Leader,* January 15, 1979

Jane Eyre
1943

DIRECTOR: Robert Stevenson; SCREENPLAY: Aldous Huxley, Robert Stevenson; CAST: Joan Fontaine, Orson Welles, Margaret O'Brien, Henry Daniell, John Sutton, Agnes Moorehead, Elizabeth Taylor.

"...a careful and tame production, a vanilla-flavored Joan Fontaine, and Welles treating himself to road-operatic sculpturings of body, cloak, and diction, his eyes glinting in the Rembrandt gloom, at every chance, like side-orders of jelly...." —James Agee, *Nation*, February 12, 1944

Juliet of the Spirits
1965

DIRECTOR: Federico Fellini; SCREENPLAY: Federico Fellini; CAST: Giulietta Masina, Mario Pisu, Sandra Milo, Valentina Cortese.

"As it turned out, Fellini missed by a mile, and I am sorry that I must write this review more in sorrow than anger, but *Juliet* is barely slick enough to pass as middlebrow entertainment on the Rose Franzblau level." —Andrew Sarris, *Village Voice*, November 11 & 18, 1965

The King of Comedy
1982

DIRECTOR: Martin Scorsese; SCREENPLAY: Paul Zimmerman; CAST: Robert De Niro, Jerry Lewis, Diahnne Abbott, Sandra Bernhard.

British Film Institute award for Best Original Screenplay.

"It's so—deliberately—quiet and empty that it doesn't provide even the dumb, mindrotting diversion that can half amuse audiences at ordinary bad movies.... *The King of Comedy* is a chore to watch, but it's much buggier and more worrying than most dead films, because its deadness must be intentional.... You can't help thinking: *The King of Comedy* is a training film for pests, and worse." —Pauline Kael, *New Yorker*, March 7, 1983

King's Row
1942

DIRECTOR: Sam Wood; SCREENPLAY: Casey Robinson, from the novel by Henry Bellamann; CAST: Ann Sheridan, Robert Cummings, Ronald Reagan, Claude Rains.

Academy Award nominations for Best Picture, Director, Cinematography.

"...the disappointing fact is that *King's Row,* as it turgidly unfolds on the screen, is one of the bulkiest blunders to come out of Hollywood in some time...*King's Row* was too much for them to hoe." —Bosley Crowther, *New York Times,* February 3, 1942

The Ladykillers
1955

DIRECTOR: Alexander Mackendrick; SCREENPLAY: William Rose; CAST: Alec Guinness, Katie Johnson, Peter Sellers, Cecil Parker, Herbert Lom.

Academy Award nomination for Best Screenplay.

"It is not really funny for the home of a gentle old lady with three parrots and a slightly wandering mind to be

invaded by five hold-up men, no matter how broadly
Guinness plays their leader. The spectator has to change
sides too much, and consequently feels a vague irrita-
tion, instead of being entertained." —Robert Kass,
Films in Review, February 1956

The Last Detail
1974

> DIRECTOR: Hal Ashby; SCREENPLAY: Robert Towne; CAST:
> Jack Nicholson, Otis Young, Randy Quaid, Clifton James,
> Carol Kane.
> Academy Award nominations for Screenplay, Best Actor,
> Supporting Actor (Randy Quaid).

"What lurks under the crust of obscenities is perhaps less
a soft heart than a soft brain....Ashby's direction is
plodding, always settling for the obvious shot, and
betraying not a hint of a personal vision. Worse yet is the
cinematography of Michael Chapman....And then there
is the blatant and banal score by Johnny Mandel."
—John Simon, *Esquire,* May 1974

Last Tango in Paris
1972

> DIRECTOR: Bernardo Bertolucci; SCREENPLAY: Bernardo
> Bertolucci; CAST: Marlon Brando, Maria Schneider, Jean-
> Pierre Léaud.
> Academy Award nominations for Director, Best Actor.

"I can no longer delay the announcement that *Last Tango
in Paris* is an utterly inconsequential picture, concerning
two of the most boring characters ever depicted on the
screen....I found the most lively character to be the

corpse of Paul's wife." —Thomas Berger, *Esquire,* May 1973

"The Last Tango is the Last Straw. It's been an age since I've heard and read such extravagant twaddle about a movie as we've had shoveled on us about *Last Tango in Paris.* This movie is the year's most over-publicized ripoff.... In many cities theaters are charging five dollars entrance fee! Now *that's* what I call obscene!" —Gene Shalit, *Ladies Home Journal,* April 1973

"It is a phony film—a romantic view of Paris, a cheap view of life, and, by God, a cheap view of filmmaking.... If you go expecting to see one of the great films of our time, you would do best to go in on a stretcher in traumatic shock, only waking up for the trailers." —Clive Barnes, *Vogue,* April 1973

"Hatred for women and a pervasive homosexual sensibility characterize the film.... The film can thus be seen as a product of the closet-queen mentality. Jeanne is...really Jean, a boy in disguise, and the filmmakers are playing with secret fears, guilt feelings, and obsessions that they want to get off their chests but dare not quite reveal.... All this, of course, is detrimental only in a film posturing as the revelation of ultimate heterosexual truths, and made by two such supermasculine men." —John Simon, *New Leader,* February 19, 1973

The Last Waltz
1978

DIRECTOR: Martin Scorsese. Documentary about the last concert of The Band.

"...all this technology to reproduce more accurately the sound of a high-powered drill inside your mouth— accompanied, worse yet, by banal words of a type that no respectable dentist's drill would be caught uttering...Even those delighted by the music (if that is what it is) should be able to see how cinematically uninteresting this event and its rendering are, despite all those cameramen and recording tracks." —John Simon, *National Review,* July 21, 1978

The Lion in Winter
1968

> DIRECTOR: Anthony Harvey; SCREENPLAY: James Goldman, from his play; CAST: Katharine Hepburn, Peter O'Toole, Jane Merrow, Anthony Hopkins, Nigel Terry.
>
> Academy Award winner for Screenplay, Score, Best Actress (Katharine Hepburn); nominations for Best Picture, Director, Actor (Peter O'Toole).

"All we have here is a nasty little struggle for power among a group of people who are all equally repugnant and among whom it is impossible for the viewer to choose even the least offensive for purposes of temporary identification....In short, *The Lion in Winter* is a mess." —Richard Schickel, from his collection *Second Sight,* 1972

"I do not want to give the director, Anthony Harvey, exclusive credit for *The Lion in Winter* debacle....First responsibility must go to James Goldman, who wrote both the original play and the screenplay....The actors can do very little with such material. Katharine Hepburn struggles valiantly and ends up a cross between Judith Anderson and Helen Hayes. *The Lion in Winter* is a

ludicrous film." —Arthur Schlesinger Jr., *Vogue,*
December 1968

Local Hero
1983

> DIRECTOR: Bill Forsyth; SCREENPLAY: Bill Forsyth; CAST: Burt
> Lancaster, Peter Riegert, Denis Lawson, Peter Capaldi,
> Fulton Mackay.
> British Academy of Film and Television Arts award for
> Best Director.

"*Local Hero* is like watching a travelogue with characters
tossed in as odd, intrusive pieces. The village architec-
ture is picturesque. The seacoast is lovely. Why did
anyone spoil it with characters and a plot that are so half-
boiled that they would be better off lost in the
moors?...Forsyth has lost his keen sense of comedy in
his new film...and the cast, including, besides Lancaster, Peter Riegert as Mac and Peter Capaldi as Oldsen, is
wasted." —Carol Olten, *San Diego Union,* April 16, 1983

Lolita
1962

> DIRECTOR: Stanley Kubrick; SCREENPLAY: Vladimir Nabokov,
> from his novel; CAST: James Mason, Shelley Winters, Sue
> Lyon, Peter Sellers.
> Academy Award nomination for Best Screenplay.

"Wind up the Lolita doll and it goes to Hollywood and
commits nymphanticide....*Lolita* is the saddest and most
important victim of the current reckless adaptation fad,
which, in sterile practice, kills the goose in order to hatch
a golden egg." —*Time,* June 22, 1962

"I'd have given the Humbert role to Peter Sellers, with perhaps Rod Steiger playing the unspeakable Quilty. That way, the central machinery of the picture might have looked less like the motel adventures of a second-hand car salesman and a quick-lunch cashier. The sex in *Lolita* is no longer perverse; it is now merely sordid."
—Robert Hatch, *Nation*, June 23, 1962

The Magnificent Seven
1960

DIRECTOR: John Sturges; SCREENPLAY: William Roberts; CAST: Yul Brynner, Steve McQueen, Robert Vaughn, James Coburn, Charles Bronson, Horst Buchholz, Eli Wallach.

"A considerable amount of money was spent on this Western—to no purpose.... A more uninteresting lot of Mexican farmers were never saved, from a gang of duller bandits by seven more unlikely gunslingers." —Ellen Fitzpatrick, *Films in Review*, November 1960

The Manchurian Candidate
1962

DIRECTOR: John Frankenheimer; SCREENPLAY: George Axelrod, from the novel by Richard Condon; CAST: Frank Sinatra, Laurence Harvey, Janet Leigh, Angela Lansbury.

Academy Award nomination for Best Supporting Actress (Angela Lansbury).

"*The Manchurian Candidate* will seem so incomprehensible you will wonder why it was made.... The screenplay is by George Axelrod.... If what he had in mind seemed to him worth doing, he should have done it better.... And the music! David Amram clearly doesn't belong in far-out company of this sort. Nor does Angela

Lansbury....Except when delivering Axelrod's nastiest cracks—nasty cracks go well with Lansbury's face—she is far less good than she has lately been, probably because she realized the film couldn't be made to come off."
—Arthur B. Clark, *Films in Review,* November 1962

Mean Streets
1973

> DIRECTOR: Martin Scorsese; SCREENPLAY: Martin Scorsese, Mardik Martin; CAST: Harvey Keitel, Robert De Niro, David Proval.

Robert De Niro and Harvey Keitel in *Mean Streets*

"What may well prove the year's most overrated film is Martin Scorsese's *Mean Streets*....The enthusiastic reception...may be due in part to its being largely child's play—and rather sloppily written, improvised, acted, photographed, and edited child's play....It could be called the Bang-Bang-You're-Dead school of filmmaking....All in all, an amateurish film; and amateurishness, in itself, is not an asset." —John Simon, *Esquire*, January 1974

Melvin and Howard
1980

> DIRECTOR: Jonathan Demme; SCREENPLAY: Bo Goldman; CAST: Paul Le Mat, Jason Robards Jr., Mary Steenburgen, Michael J. Pollard.
>
> Academy Award winner for Screenplay, Best Supporting Actress (Mary Steenburgen); nominations for Supporting Actor (Jason Robards Jr.).

"Between the beginning and the end comes about 80 percent of the picture, in which there is nothing but Melvin's life; and Melvin isn't very engrossing....The very poverty of the script betrays the false emphasis, the willingness to settle for Melvin's diddly doings as most of the story. Imagine a film about Mr. Deeds before he inherits the money and goes to town." —Stanley Kauffmann, *New Republic*, November 8, 1980

National Lampoon's Vacation
1983

> DIRECTOR: Harold Ramis; SCREENPLAY: John Hughes; CAST: Chevy Chase, Imogene Coca, Beverly D'Angelo, Randy Quaid.

"...not even impeccably pedigreed comics such as Chevy Chase, Imogene Coca, and John Candy can do more than competently mug their way through John Hughes's tasteless script." —Mark Czarnecki, *Macleans,* August 15, 1983

"The tastelessness would not matter, I suppose, if the jokes were funny." —Robert Asahina, *New Leader,* September 19, 1983

"...like many a long, hot car journey the vistas and the changing cityscapes tend after a while to induce a sleepy indifference..." —John Pym, *Monthly Film Bulletin,* November 1983

"...the gags are often obvious, and most of the vulgarity seems tacked on, like a sop to current fashion that even the filmmakers don't care much about. And who's responsible for all the racist attitudes?...Next time, National Lampoon, how about roasting racism off the screen instead of treating it like an old pal?" —David Sterritt, *Christian Science Monitor,* September 15, 1983

"*National Lampoon's Vacation* is no day at the beach. Indeed, they don't come much worse than this desperately frenetic, tiresomely predictable, insufferably simple-minded farce....Randy Quaid, Eugene Levy, John Candy, and Brian Doyle-Murray are among the supporting players who could be sued for nonsupport." —Joe Leydon, *Houston Post,* July 29, 1983

"Only one thing works consistently in *National Lampoon's Vacation,* which opens today. Unfortunately, it's the camera." —Stephen Hunter, *Baltimore Sun,* July 29, 1983

"By the time *National Lampoon's Vacation*...approaches its finish, its underlying point that Americans tend to

become desperate in their grim determination to have fun becomes clear. But it's long been invalidated by all the uninspired garbage that has gone before it. Everyone involved would have been better off staying home."
—Kevin Thomas, *Los Angeles Times,* July 29, 1983

Network
1976

DIRECTOR: Sidney Lumet; SCREENPLAY: Paddy Chayevsky; CAST: Peter Finch, William Holden, Faye Dunaway, Robert Duvall, Wesley Addy, Ned Beatty, Beatrice Straight.

Academy Award winner for Best Screenplay, Actor (Peter Finch), Actress (Faye Dunaway), Supporting Actress (Beatrice Straight); nominations for Best Picture, Director, Cinematography, Actor (William Holden), Supporting Actor (Ned Beatty).

"For all the self-consciously deployed 25-cent words in its screenplay, this movie is so heavy-handed and simplistic that a 12-year-old wouldn't find it challenging.... It's embarrassing to watch a film try so hard to be daring and fall so flat.... Lumet's direction meanwhile is as disheveled as the script." —Frank Rich, *New York Post,* November 15, 1976

"*Network* borders so obviously on the banal and trivial in dealing with life at the top, network division, that it defeats all its good parts, overcomes its own heart and should make a dandy sit-com in the 1978–1979 season."
—Bill Granger, *Chicago Sun-Times,* December 16, 1976

Oliver!
1968

DIRECTOR: Carol Reed; SCREENPLAY: Vernon Harris, from the play by Lionel Bart and the novel by Charles Dickens; CAST: Ron Moody, Oliver Reed, Harry Secombe, Mark Lester.

Academy Award for Best Picture, Director, Musical Direction; nominations for Screenplay, Cinematography, Actor, Supporting Actor.

"I don't like any of Lionel Bart's songs or any of the singers, and I don't appreciate the rather disquieting spectacle of a horde of pint-sized chorus boys doing Jerome Robbins imitations in the midst of fustian melodramatics. As for Ron Moody's fey Fagin, his school-of-hard-knocks song spiels remind me of nothing so much as Zorba the Fiddler from La Mancha, that all-purpose monster of middle-class, middle-aged, middlebrow metaphysics." —Andrew Sarris, *Village Voice,* January 9, 1969

Orpheus (*Orphée*)
1949

DIRECTOR: Jean Cocteau; SCREENPLAY: Jean Cocteau; CAST: Jean Marais, François Périer, Maria Casarès.

"It's more Morpheus than Orpheus by us." —Bosley Crowther, *New York Times,* November 30, 1950

The Pink Panther _____
1964

> DIRECTOR: Blake Edwards; SCREENPLAY: Maurice Richlin,
> Blake Edwards; CAST: David Niven, Peter Sellers, Capucine,
> Claudia Cardinale, Robert Wagner.

"In addition to threadbare material there is a very poor performance by Peter Sellers as a French police inspector....Sellers seemed so at a loss in this role that he resorted to bumping into things, knocking things over, etc., to get laughs....As for Robert Wagner, who plays Niven's nephew, he is losing his looks and has not acquired the acting ability which would hide it."
—Georges Millau, *Films in Review,* May 1964

Portrait of Jennie _____
1948

> DIRECTOR: William Dieterle; SCREENPLAY: Peter Berneis, Paul
> Osborn, Leonard Bernovici; CAST: Jennifer Jones, Joseph
> Cotten, Ethel Barrymore, David Wayne, Lillian Gish, Henry
> Hull.

"Allowing for some lovely glimpses of New York and winter in Central Park and a fairly respectable performance of a picture dealer by Ethel Barrymore, the remaining aspects and actors, including Lillian Gish and David Wayne, are substantially the same as the whole thing, which is deficient and disappointing in the extreme."   —Bosley Crowther, *New York Times,* March 30, 1949

Rebel Without a Cause —————————————
1955

DIRECTOR: Nicholas Ray; SCREENPLAY: Stewart Stern; CAST: James Dean, Natalie Wood, Sal Mineo, Dennis Hopper.

Selected to the National Film Registry, Library of Congress. Academy Award nominations for Original Story, Supporting Actress (Natalie Wood), Best Supporting Actor (Sal Mineo).

"The thing that eats off the current crop, we are in-formed, is the fact that they don't get enough love, from their parents, but their conduct would indicate that what really ails them is the lack of some sound discipline. At any rate, they are a terrible lot, and their notion of fun and games...becomes tedious as time goes by....In the two hours it takes *Rebel Without a Cause* to exhaust itself, time goes by slowly." —John McCarten, *New Yorker,* November 5, 1955

Repulsion —————————————————
1965

DIRECTOR: Roman Polanski; SCREENPLAY: Roman Polanski, Gerard Brach; CAST: Catherine Deneuve, Ian Hendry, John Fraser.

"This morbid thriller by the young Polish director Roman Polanski...should have been subtitled 'Homage to Hitchcock,' because that is what it is and what is wrong with it...*Repulsion* is such a serious picture that it threatens constantly to become a silly one." —Brendan Gill, *New Yorker,* October 9, 1965

Requiem for a Heavyweight ————————————
1962

DIRECTOR: Ralph Nelson; SCREENPLAY: Rod Serling, from his
teleplay; CAST: Anthony Quinn, Jackie Gleason, Mickey
Rooney, Julie Harris.

"Rod Serling's expansion of his television playlet into an
84-minute film has all the speciousness of so much of his
work. Even interesting performances by Anthony Quinn
and Jackie Gleason do not redeem it. The fight racket is
a dreary business at best and Serling is here intent on
making it drearier." —Wilfred Mifflin, *Films in Review*,
November 1962

Rosemary's Baby ————————————————
1968

DIRECTOR: Roman Polanski; Screenplay; Roman Polanski,
from the novel by Ira Levin; CAST: Mia Farrow, John
Cassavetes, Ruth Gordon, Sidney Blackmer.

"I was aware, as the film unreeled, that Messrs. Levin
and Polanski were latching on to the witchcraft revival
currently being stirred up by perverts.... To my surprise,
I have since encountered people who allege *Rosemary's
Baby* is not about the delusions women nurture before
and after they give birth, but is actually, and seriously,
about witches." —H.H., *Films in Review*, August/Sep-
tember 1968

"Nothing about this film suggests the talent that once
gave us *Knife in the Water* and *Two Men and a Wardrobe*; the
few vaguely suspenseful moments could have been made
by any reasonably competent hack...." —John Simon,
New Leader, August 8, 1968

The Seven Year Itch ———————————————————
1955

DIRECTOR: Billy Wilder; SCREENPLAY: Billy Wilder, George
Axelrod, from his play; CAST: Tom Ewell, Marilyn Monroe,
Sonny Tufts, Oscar Homolka.

"As the once-amusing story drags on and on endlessly
and Tom acts more and more like a fool, one begins to
think the whole thing should have been called the seven
year picture." —Philip T. Hartung, *Commonweal*, June
24, 1955

"...offers several stimulating views of Marilyn Monroe
as a substitute for the comedy that George Axelrod got
into the original version of this trifle. True, there are
occasions when Tom Ewell provokes a laugh or two as a
husband who, in the absence of his wife, finds himself
preoccupied with extramarital fantasies, but when Miss
Monroe turns up as a young lady too substantial for
dreams, the picture is reduced to the level of a burlesque
show, and Mr. Ewell's efforts to be quietly funny are lost
in the shuffle." —John McCarten, *New Yorker*, June 11,
1955

"...the entire film continually misses fire and fizzles out,
like defective fireworks. And the chief reason, doubtless,
is Marilyn Monroe's radiant presence. She is as out of
place in a sophisticated comedy as she would be in a
Tibetan lamasery, or, to be more exact, in a nunnery. She
has been profoundly miscast." —Delmore Schwartz,
New Republic, August 8, 1955

"The hilarity of *The Seven Year Itch* escapes me....Of
course the whole thing can be looked on as a feverish
reverie, the average American male's daydream, com-

pounded of overwork, anxiety, and the blandishments of modern beer advertising. In that case, it is certainly not funny." —Robert Hatch, *Nation,* June 25, 1955

"The Seven Year Itch is, as far as I am concerned, painfully offensive and unfunny....casting Marilyn Monroe as the uninhibited lassie upstairs destroyed what pretensions to respectability the play had. With Marilyn in the part, the picture is not satirizing sex but peddling it." —Moira Walsh, *America,* June 25, 1955

sex, lies, and videotape
1989

> DIRECTOR: Steven Soderbergh; SCREENPLAY: Steven Soderbergh; CAST: James Spader, Andie MacDowell, Peter Gallagher, Laura San Giacomo.
> Academy Award nomination for Best Original Screenplay.

"...about as schematic, shallow, and insufferably dinky as a movie can get...If a picture as starved for substance and originality (and incidentally, erotic gratification)...can luck into the grand prize at the Cannes Film Festival and earn its self-evidently groping and tentative creator, 26-year-old Steven Soderbergh, an instantly inflated reputation as prodigy of the moment, then outrageous good fortune could smile on all of us." —Gary Arnold, *Washington Times,* August 11, 1989

She Wore a Yellow Ribbon
1949

> DIRECTOR: John Ford; SCREENPLAY: Frank Nugent, Laurence Stallings; CAST: John Wayne, Joanne Dru, John Agar, Ben Johnson.
> Academy Award for Cinematography.

"For some unaccountable reason the hair-raising possibilities of authentic history have been submerged in the
muddled and often maudlin story....a sad waste of talent
and Technicolor." —*Time*, October 24, 1949

"Compared with Mr. Ford's major effort along these
lines—*Stagecoach*—this one is, I'm afraid, completely
unremarkable." —John McCarten, *New Yorker*,
December 3, 1949

Shoeshine
1946

> DIRECTOR: Vittorio De Sica; SCREENPLAY: Cesare Zavattini,
> Sergio Amidei, Adolfo Franci, C. G. Viola; CAST: Franco
> Interlenghi, Rinaldo Smordoni.
> Winner of Special Academy Award; nomination for Best
> Screenplay.

"A senselessly grim ending and the depiction of bru-
talities which seem more an exercise of the director's
whim than an integral part of the story rob *Shoeshine* of
its laurels....Patrons who enjoy beating themselves may
take a shine to it—but masochism as b.o. lure is a
doubtful quantity." —*Variety*, August 13, 1947

Stand by Me
1986

> DIRECTOR: Rob Reiner; SCREENPLAY: Raynold Gideon and
> others, from the story "The Body," by Stephen King; CAST:
> Will Wheaton, River Phoenix, Corey Feldman, Jerry
> O'Connell, Kiefer Sutherland, Richard Dreyfuss.

"Rarely have 90 minutes of screen time been devoted to
anything more trivial or pointless....Although nothing

of any consequence happens to anybody in *Stand by Me,* the kid with the big imagination passes the time by telling the other kids stories. This gives Rob Reiner a chance to stage a fantasy scene that should win some kind of award for ultimate tastelessness...." —Rex Reed, *New York Post,* August 8, 1986

"*Stand by Me* is a shuck. It trumpets its sensitivity while reveling in coarseness. And at its climax it suggests that manhood can be found through the barrel of a gun. Maybe this how Rambo discovered puberty. Maybe real kids should be discouraged, from following his example." —Richard Corliss, *Time,* August 25, 1986

Stolen Kisses (*Baissers volés*)
1968

> DIRECTOR: François Truffaut; SCREENPLAY: François Truffaut, Claude de Givray, Bernard Revon; CAST: Jean-Pierre Léaud, Delphine Seyrig, Michel Lonsdale.
>
> Academy Award nomination for Best Foreign Film.

"...drags its audience down into his own creamy satin-pillowed memory of lyrical innocence-gone-astray that quite frankly doesn't seem worth the bother. Only the French could feel all washed up at 37; if Truffaut makes any more movies like this one, I'm going to start believing him. *Stolen Kisses* makes what's left of the New Wave seem distinctly Old Drizzle." —Rex Reed, from his collection *Big Screen, Little Screen,* 1971

A Streetcar Named Desire
1951

> DIRECTOR: Elia Kazan; SCREENPLAY: Tennessee Williams, from his play; CAST: Vivien Leigh, Marlon Brando, Kim Hunter, Karl Malden.

Academy Award winner for Best Actress (Vivien Leigh), Supporting Actress (Kim Hunter), Supporting Actor (Karl Malden); nominations for Best Picture, Screenplay, Director, Cinematography, Score, Actor (Marlon Brando), Art Direction.

"Everything that kept the Broadway *Streetcar*, from spinning off into ridiculous melodrama—everything thoughtful, muted, three-dimensional—has been raped,

Marlon Brando and Vivian Leigh in *A Streetcar Named Desire*

along with poor Blanche Dubois, in the Hollywood version.... Brando, having fallen hard for the critics' idea that Stanley is simply animal and slob, now screams and postures and sweeps plates off the table with an ape-like emphasis that unfortunately becomes predictable." —Manny Farber, *Nation*, October 20, 1951

The Stunt Man _____
1980

> DIRECTOR: Richard Rush; SCREENPLAY: Lawrence B. Marcus, from a novel by Paul Brodeur; CAST: Peter O'Toole, Steve Railsback, Barbara Hershey.
>
> Academy Award nominations for Best Screenplay, Director, Actor (Peter O'Toole).

"Felicity is not in Richard Rush, the director. Even with the script's big and little defects, his film might be tolerable if it weren't so portentous and mannered.... no tenfold-better script could survive this heavy treatment. No twofold-better director would be suckered by it.... O, O'Toole, if only you chose better scripts!" —Stanley Kauffmann, *New Republic*, November 8, 1980

The Sweet Smell of Success _____ _
1957

> DIRECTOR: Alexander Mackendrick; SCREENPLAY: Clifford Odets, Ernest Lehman; CAST: Burt Lancaster, Tony Curtis, Martin Milner.
>
> Selected to the National Film Registry, Library of Congress.

"Don't think you won't find things to watch, movie music to get heart attacks from, camera work to keep you dazed and screaming. It's the New Technique (circa 1950) come to full flower—and almost total meaninglessness." — Jerry Tallmer, *Village Voice*, August 28, 1957

"If you could believe it, it would be a real shocker; but if you could believe it, you would not be going around without an attendant.... The weather is hot, the space is limited and nothing is to be gained by describing exactly how this picture is ridiculous. It is not about people— that is ridiculous enough." —Robert Hatch, *Nation*, July 20, 1957

"*The Sweet Smell of Success* has the taste of ashes." —Arthur Knight, *Saturday Review*, July 6, 1957

"One of the most cynical movies ever made...*Sweet Smell* doesn't answer any questions and it doesn't smell very sweet." —Philip T. Hartung, *Commonweal*, July 12, 1957

Taxi Driver
1976

> DIRECTOR: Martin Scorsese; SCREENPLAY: Paul Schrader;
> CAST: Robert De Niro, Jodie Foster, Cybill Shepherd, Peter Boyle, Leonard Harris, Harvey Keitel.
> Academy Award nominations for Best Picture, Score, Actor (Robert De Niro), Supporting Actress (Jodie Foster).

"De Niro, one of our finest young actors, is totally wasted.... *Taxi Driver* is neither entertainment or art. It is a rambling, unfocused, one-dimensional wallow in cheap sensationalism." —Marcia Magill, *Films in Review*, March 1976

"After seeing *Taxi Driver*, you'll think twice before hailing a cab. You also will think twice about the integrity of a

movie that begins impressively as it shapes the inarticu-
lated disorder, aggression, and isolation in a man and
concludes like so many other pictures that had nothing
to say after all—with ghoulishness, some facile irony, and
a cutesy-pie twist. . . . That the film, with so much going
for it early on, turns into a hack job can only be blamed
on Scorsese." —Rena Andrews, *Denver Post*, February
26, 1976

The Tin Drum
1979

> DIRECTOR: Volker Schlöndorff; SCREENPLAY: Jean-Claude
> Carrière, Franz Seitz, Volker Schlöndorff, from the novel by
> Günter Grass; CAST: David Bennent, Mario Adorf, Angela
> Winkler, Daniel Olbrychski.
> Academy Award winner for Best Foreign Film.

"...a sublime specimen of Classic Comix...It is fitting
that the little (and diminished) Oskar should have won
Hollywood's Oscar. Midget to midget: an Oskar who
won't grow up and has shrunk further on film, and an
Oscar that dependably rewards the puny and immature." —John Simon, from his collection *Something to
Declare*, 1983.

To Be or Not to Be
1942

> DIRECTOR: Ernst Lubitsch; SCREENPLAY: Edwin Justus Mayer;
> CAST: Jack Benny, Carole Lombard, Robert Stack.

"There is just enough of the reality of Warsaw burning
and the persecution of the Poles—and Lubitsch goes out
of his way to include a solemn moment or two of

commentary—to make the farcical high spirits of the rest seem an offence against taste and the film itself an artistic blunder." —*London Times*, April 30, 1942

To Kill a Mockingbird
1962

DIRECTOR: Robert Mulligan; SCREENPLAY: Horton Foote, from the novel by Harper Lee; CAST: Gregory Peck, Mary Badham, Philip Alford.

Academy Award winner for Best Screenplay, Actor (Gregory Peck); nominations for Best Picture, Director, Cinematography, Score, Supporting Actress (Mary Badham).

"*To Kill a Mockingbird* relates the Cult of Childhood to the Negro Problem with disastrous results. Before the intellectual confusion of the project is considered, it should be noted that this is not much of a movie even by purely formal standards." —Andrew Sarris, *Village Voice*, March 7, 1963

The Trouble With Harry
1955

DIRECTOR: Alfred Hitchcock; SCREENPLAY: John Michael Hayes; CAST: Edmund Gwenn, Mildred Natwick, John Forsythe, Shirley Maclaine.

"What the picture does have in its favor are the Vermont backgrounds, beautifully photographed in VistaVision and Technicolor, but they do not make up for the plot's dullness or the *doubles entendres*. Maybe the trouble with Harry is Alfred." —Philip T. Hartung, *Commonweal*, November 11, 1955

Tunes of Glory ————————————————
1960

> DIRECTOR: Ronald Neame; SCREENPLAY: James Kennaway,
> from his novel; CAST: Alec Guinness, John Mills, Susannah
> York.
> Academy Award nomination for Best Screenplay.

"Pleasanter expectations were never so flaccidly dashed.
We get a drama of character, but we do not care very
much about the characters, which are ineptly and inade-
quately characterized, nor about their rather unnecessary dilemmas. The fault is largely in the script.... We
are aware all too soon that the story is factitious and will
fall apart, and an inexplicable suicide at the end is the
crowning ineptitude. The acting is also a disappointment." —Ellen Fitzpatrick, *Films in Review,* January
1961

Two for the Road ————————————————
1966

> DIRECTOR: Stanley Donen; SCREENPLAY: Frederic Raphael;
> CAST: Albert Finney, Audrey Hepburn.
> Academy Award nomination for Best Screenplay.

"Raphael has written an impressive screenplay.... Donen
was not the man to direct it, though.... He has ruined
every moment of Raphael's screenplay; he has trans-
formed it into a slick fiction of stunning images that
looks like mere posturing.... Audrey Hepburn fits easily
into Donen's style: she is merely another dazzling object
to linger on." —Raymond Banacki, *Film Quarterly,*
Summer 1967

Ugetsu Monogatari
1953

DIRECTOR: Kenji Mizoguchi; SCREENPLAY: Matsutaro
Kawaguchi; CAST: Masayuki Mori, Machiko Kyo, Sakae
Ozawa, Mitsuko Mito.
Grand Prize winner at the Venice Film Festival.

"...it contains more writhing and tumbling than has
been seen since the Keystone Cops turned in their
badges...that Japanese acting is such a violent combination of heavy breathing and emotional contortions that
it's hard to reconcile with Lafcadio Hearn, the flower
arrangements, and all that. The plot of *Ugetsu* is pretty
badly contorted, too, and often incomprehensible."
—John McCarten, *New Yorker,* September 18, 1954

The Virgin Spring (*Jungfrukällan*)
1959

DIRECTOR: Ingmar Bergman; SCREENPLAY: Ulla Isaakson;
CAST: Max Von Sydow, Brigitta Valberg, Gunnel Lindblom,
Brigitta Pettersson.
Academy Award winner for Best Foreign Film.

"Ingmar Bergman's latest is a hastily and carelessly made
film....In Europe it acquired notoriety because of a
sexsational rape scene, two minutes of which have been
cut, from the print that will be shown here. Shorn of that
dubious asset, *The Virgin Spring* has nothing for sensa-
tion-seekers, and very little for anyone else, including
Bergmaniacs." —Helen Weldon Kuhn, *Films in Review,*
November 1960

White Heat
1949

> DIRECTOR: Raoul Walsh; SCREENPLAY: Ivan Goff, Ben
> Roberts, from a story by Virginia Kellogg; CAST: James
> Cagney, Edmond O'Brien, Margaret Wycherly, Virginia
> Mayo.

"*White Heat* follows the new style in cinema violence....As usual, the moral that crime doesn't pay is
somewhat overshadowed by the fact that it is made to
look attractively exciting...made me wonder if Hollywood's bloodbaths may not be infectious on prolonged
contact." —Robert Hatch, *New Republic*, September 26,
1949

Wings of Desire (*Der Himmel über Berlin*)
1987

> DIRECTOR: Wim Wenders; SCREENPLAY: Wim Wenders, Peter
> Handke; CAST: Bruno Ganz, Solveig Dommartin, Otto
> Sander, Curt Bois, Peter Falk.
> Cannes Film Festival winner for Best Director.

"...denatured, spiritless and dull...*Wings of Desire* is a
lifeless, joyless film, a film without memory set in a city
without memory." —Barbara Shulgasser, *San Francisco
Examiner*, June 10, 1988

"The underlying conception of *Wings of Desire* is enchanting, but Mr. Wenders allows it to become terribly over-
ripe....The excesses of language, the ceaseless camera
movement, the unyielding whimsy have the ultimate
effect of wearing the audience down." —Janet Maslin,
New York Times, April 29, 1988

"It's a sluggish, weary-winged fable; it seems to be saying that if you're a grownup living in postwar Germany a reminder of childish joy is the most you can hope for....Sentimentality and meaninglessness: postmodern kitsch." —Pauline Kael, *New Yorker*, May 30, 1988

A Woman Under the Influence _____
1974

> DIRECTOR: John Cassavetes; SCREENPLAY: John Cassavetes; CAST: Peter Falk, Gena Rowlands.
> Selected to the National Film Registy, Library of Congress. Academy Award nominations for Best Director, Actress (Gena Rowlands).

"...this film is utterly without interest or merit..." —Stanley Kauffmann, *New Republic*, December 28, 1974

"I would just as gladly have passed over the dreadful *A Woman Under the Influence* in condign silence, but the success it begins to garner calls for a cry of protest....A dreary little situation is stretched, worried, reiterated until any spectator with a sense of the value of his time must turn as blue in the face as the hero's collar." —John Simon, *Esquire*, April 1975

Zorba the Greek _____
1964

> DIRECTOR: Michael Cacoyannis; SCREENPLAY: Michael Cacoyannis; CAST: Anthony Quinn, Alan Bates, Lila Kedrova, Irene Papas
> Academy Award winner for Cinematography, Best Supporting Actress (Lila Kedrova); nominations for Best Picture, Screenplay, Director, Actor (Anthony Quinn).

"*Zorba the Greek* is quite a bad film.... Amid the purifying scenery of Crete this tainted production slowly unfolds.... The manner of execution is as fixed as an aria, and neither Quinn nor the director, Michael Cacoyannis, has invented so much as a fresh trill." —Elizabeth Hardwick, *Vogue*, February 15, 1965

About the Authors

ARDIS SILLICK received her master's degree in library science from the University of Iowa. She worked eleven years at a public library reference desk and lived to tell about it. Her taste in movies tends toward what might kindly be described as the offbeat. "Some of my favorite movies are ones the critics (and most everyone else) dismissed offhand," she says. Ardis recently completed work on a database that includes acting, production, and music credits for over 21,000 films. She lives near Toledo, Iowa. This is her first book.

MICHAEL MCCORMICK graduated from the University of Iowa with a degree in film and broadcasting. For most of his life he has divided his time between Seattle and his family's farm in Iowa. His work as an extra and stand-in for Clu Gulager in the 1974 John Wayne epic *McQ* remains the apex of his movie career (so far). Says Mike: "I remember the time I saw Roger Ebert give 'thumbs up' to *Benji the Hunted* but 'thumbs down' to Stanley Kubrick's *Full Metal Jacket*. That was the last time I paid much attention to his opinion." This is his first book.